SUPER
FAST

INSTANT POT
PRESSURE COOKER
COOKBOOK

SUPER FAST

INSTANT POT PRESSURE ····COOKER····

COOKBOOK

100 EASY RECIPES FOR EVERY MULTI-COOKER

HEATHER RODINO
& ELLA SANDERS

Castle Point Books
New York

CONTENTS

INTRODUCTION

Electric pressure-cooking has taken the nation by storm. And why not? Compared to the stovetop or the oven, an electric pressure cooker is less messy, generates less heat (a boon in summer), uses less electricity, and retains more vitamins in the food. Dishes that would normally take hours to cook—tough cuts of meat, dried beans—take minutes. And it's easier than a traditional stovetop pressure cooker because you don't have to adjust the heat levels. If you're a busy family, a working couple, a budget- or health-conscious cook, and even regardless of whether or not you like to cook, an electric pressure cooker has something to offer you.

The goal of *Super Fast Instant Pot Pressure Cooker Cookbook* is to give you 100 electric pressure-cooker recipes you can get on the table in sixty minutes or less—often much less—from start to finish, including prep time. (Okay, there are one or two exceptions. Did someone mention cheesecake?) And most of that hour will be free time when the machine is working hard to make you a delicious meal. While there are thousands of non–pressure cooker recipes you can make in under 30 minutes, the idea here is to make accessible dishes that might take a little—or a lot—longer if you made them conventionally. Most of the electric pressure cookers, also known as multi-cookers, on the market can do many things: make yogurt and rice, slow-cook, and steam. The only thing they can't seem to do is wash themselves or take out the trash! This book focuses exclusively on the "Manual" pressure-cooking function, though we'll also use "Sauté" to brown foods. If your pot does not have a sauté or similar setting, you can perform the same function with a pan on the stovetop.

If you're new to pressure cooking, you may have been drawn in by enticing claims of having dinner on the table in two minutes or ten minutes. Well, yes and no. A pressure cooker takes some time to come up to pressure *before* the cooking time starts. This process usually takes about ten minutes or so—much longer if you're cooking something from frozen (and yes, you can do that too, unlike with a slow-cooker). Only then does the cooking time begin, and the machine counts down from there. After the cooking time is over, the pot is still pressurized. (Don't even *think* about trying to open the lid at this point.) The pressure releases in one of two ways, either naturally, meaning you just wait until the float valve drops and it's safe to open the lid (a process that takes between ten and twenty minutes), or you manually release the pressure by turning the steam release knob. Many recipes in this book use a partial natural release of five, ten, or fifteen minutes, followed by a manual release to release any remaining pressure. During a manual release, the machine will start shooting hot steam from the knob, so you'll want to protect your hands with an oven or silicone mitt before you turn the knob. (Check out the owner's manual of your particular multi-cooker for guidance on how this function works on your pot.) So essentially, **pressure-building time + cook time + pressure-releasing time = total cook time.** This means the stovetop or oven is still a better bet for foods that are delicate or cook quickly (such as seafood or pasta), but there are a few exceptions to this rule. In the case of steel-cut oats, for example, the total cook time is about the same as the stovetop, but it's just so much easier to make them in the pressure cooker because you don't have to monitor or stir them.

Thus, while the multi-cooker is not exactly instant, it is pretty darn fast, making a dish that might have taken two hours to cook on the stovetop doable in twenty to thirty minutes of pressure time (forty to fifty minutes from start to finish). For many people, however, the real beauty of electric pressure-cooking may be that *you don't have to do anything to it while it's cooking*. That may sound obvious, but even with a pot of something long-simmering on the stove, you still have to stir occasionally. For food that's roasting in the oven, you have to check on it, make sure it's not burning, baste it, turn it, and so on. Initially, it might feel a little strange to "set it and forget it"—and especially if you're an avid cook, it is indeed a bit of a leap of faith to use an electric pressure cooker, because you can't see inside to know how your food is progressing. You start it and it's all a mystery until it beeps, the pressure releases, and you lift the lid. Sort of scary—and yet entirely liberating. In the meantime, you can make a salad, get a pot of rice or pasta going, help the kids with homework, start a load of laundry, catch up on email, or simply relax. (Just don't stray *too* far away!) If you're preparing multiple courses, the pressure cooker allows you to nearly forget about one them. If you're making a complicated main course on the stovetop, get an easy side dish going in the pot. Before you know it, you'll wonder how you ever managed without your multi-cooker.

A FEW TIPS

In this book, for the purposes of calculating the "Total Time" a recipe will take, ten minutes have been built in as the time it takes the pot to reach pressure. Your individual pot may take more or less time than this.

✳ Many pots switch to a "Keep Warm" function after the cook time is over. To avoid overcooking, press Cancel or unplug the pot. If you are doing a partial natural release—where you let the pot release pressure naturally for a number of minutes before manually releasing any remaining pressure—you'll need a timer to keep track of how much time has elapsed.

✳ Don't overfill the pot. For foods that expand during cooking, like beans, don't fill it more than half full. For other foods, don't fill it more than two-thirds full.

✳ When you open the lid, open it away from yourself and others. Similarly, when you release the pressure, keep your hands and face away from the hot steam.

✳ This introduction is not a substitute for reading and understanding the owner's manual of your pot. Read it and refer back to it from time to time because we all forget stuff! There are lots of brands and models of electric pressure cookers on the market now and more arriving all the time, and each one takes some getting used to. Get to know the different parts, how to keep them clean, and how to use your pot safely. You may find that your pot cooks a little slower or faster than what the recipe indicates. Adapt the cooking time accordingly. Be patient, and you'll find the small initial learning curve was worth it for how much ease the pot brings to your life.

TROUBLESHOOTING

Too much liquid. Pressure cookers require a certain amount of liquid to come up to pressure. The amount varies by model, but it's generally between one and two cups. In addition, the cooking method itself forces foods to release a lot of their liquid, and unlike stovetop cooking, not much of that liquid is lost through evaporation. This means that when you open the lid, there may be a lot more liquid in the pot than you were expecting. To reduce your sauce and concentrate its flavor, simmer the liquid for a few minutes until it reaches the desired consistency. If your dish includes a meat that can be easily overcooked (like chicken breast), remove it to a plate before you reduce the sauce. (On the other hand, dried foods, like rice, dried beans, and dried fruit, will absorb liquid, so make sure you include enough.)

The pot won't come up to pressure. Check to make sure that the steam release handle has been switched to "sealing" and that you've included enough liquid.

Something other than steam comes out of the steam release handle. Quickly turn the handle to the sealing position and allow the pressure to release naturally. It's possible that foam has built up inside the pot or that the pot is overfilled. Be sure to clean it thoroughly afterwards to avoid any blockages. Certain foods, such as oatmeal and other starchy or dehydrated items, require a natural release. Refer to your owner's manual for more information.

Smelly silicone sealing ring. The silicone ring tends to absorb cooking odors. Remove and wash it after every use, and let it dry thoroughly. If you are particularly bothered by the smell, you can use separate rings for sweet and savory dishes.

USEFUL TOOLS AND EQUIPMENT

The multi-cooker comes with a steam rack, but there are few other items you'll want to have on hand.

A **timer** is helpful for keeping track of how much time has elapsed after the cooking process is over, so you know when to release the pressure. While many pots have a "keep warm" function that will show digitally how many minutes have elapsed since the end of the cook time, it's easy to overcook foods this way, so it's better to shut the pot off and/or unplug it.

· ·

An **instant-read thermometer** will ensure that meats and other foods have reached a safe minimum cooking temperature.

· ·

A **6- or 7-inch springform pan or baking pan with removable bottom** is ideal for making cheesecake in the electric pressure cooker.

· ·

A **high-sided 7-inch round baking pan or soufflé dish** for recipes that require you to use a pan inside the pot.

· ·

Foil sling. Take a sheet of aluminum foil about 18 to 20 inches long. Fold the two long sides toward the center to make a long sling. You'll use this to carefully lower in and remove cookware from the multicooker. Tuck in the ends before closing the lid.

· ·

Steam basket. A simple stainless-steel collapsible steam basket makes cooking potatoes, squash, and other vegetables a cinch and keeps them from falling through the steam rack. Place it on top of the steam rack.

· ·

Silicone baking mitt(s). Wear these when releasing the pressure valve to protect yourself from the steam. Also useful when removing the inner pot.

· ·

STARTERS AND SOUPS

SMOKY DEVILED EGGS

Smoky Deviled Eggs swaps out regular paprika for its smoked cousin. Sometimes called *pimentón*, smoked paprika can usually be found next to the regular paprika at the supermarket. If you can't find it, you can use regular sweet or hot paprika, or even substitute a teaspoon of chopped canned chipotle for a smoky *and* spicy alternative. **MAKES 12**

ACTIVE TIME: 10 minutes **PRESSURE TIME:** 5 minutes
RELEASE METHOD: Manual **TOTAL TIME:** 25 minutes

---

6 large eggs

3 tablespoons mayonnaise

1 pinch cayenne pepper

¼ teaspoon black pepper

1 teaspoon Dijon mustard

2 tablespoons chopped chives

Smoked paprika, for garnish

1. Pour 2 cups of water into the inner pot and insert the steam rack. Carefully place the eggs on the steam rack.

2. Lock the lid. Cook on high pressure for 5 minutes, then manually release the pressure.

3. While the eggs are cooking, mix together the mayonnaise, cayenne, black pepper, and mustard in a small bowl.

4. Transfer the eggs to a bowl of ice water. When cool enough to handle, peel them, slice them in half, and remove the yolks.

5. Add the yolks to the mayonnaise mixture and mash them gently with a fork until evenly combined.

6. Spoon the yolk mixture into the egg white halves, and sprinkle with chives and smoked paprika.

SMART TIP: To keep the eggs from rolling around, crumple up small balls of aluminum foil and place them in the pot between each egg.

TEXAS CAVIAR

If you've never heard of Texas Caviar, it's a delicious marinated bean dip usually made with black-eyed peas. A great make-ahead dish for a party, this recipe tastes even better the next day. Don't even bother to soak the black-eyed peas overnight, as it only shortens the cooking time by only two minutes! **SERVES 6 TO 8**

ACTIVE TIME: 15 minutes PRESSURE TIME: 7 minutes RELEASE METHOD: Natural (15 minutes) TOTAL TIME: 45 minutes (plus refrigerating time)

½ pound dried black-eyed peas, rinsed and picked over for debris

1 tablespoon olive oil

Kosher salt

1 red bell pepper, seeded and chopped

1 green bell pepper, seeded and chopped

1 rib celery, chopped

1 (8.75-ounce) can corn, drained

3 scallions, white and green parts, thinly sliced

1 jalapeño pepper, seeded and minced

¾ cup bottled Italian dressing

2 tablespoons chopped fresh cilantro

2 tablespoons chopped fresh parsley

2 Hass avocados, cubed (see Smart Tip)

1. Place the black-eyed peas in the inner pot with enough water to cover by at least one inch. Stir in the oil and ½ teaspoon of salt.

2. Lock the lid. Cook on high pressure for 7 minutes. Let the pressure release naturally for 15 minutes, then manually release any remaining pressure. Drain the beans in a colander, and let cool slightly.

3. Meanwhile, in a large bowl, stir together the bell peppers, celery, corn, scallion, jalapeño, and Italian dressing. Fold in the beans, cilantro, parsley, and avocado.

4. Refrigerate before serving. Serve with tortilla chips.

SMART TIP: If you're making Texas Caviar the day before you plan to serve it, wait until the last minute to add the avocados to avoid browning.

SWEET CHILI WINGS

Sweet Chili Wings are a twist on traditional Buffalo wings. They are infused with ginger, garlic, and soy sauce before being browned and crisped under the broiler and tossed with mildly hot sweet chili sauce. To amp up the heat, drizzle the wings with a little sriracha sauce before serving. **MAKES 24**

ACTIVE TIME: 10 minutes **PRESSURE TIME:** 10 minutes
RELEASE METHOD: Manual **TOTAL TIME:** 30 minutes

---

1 cup chicken stock

2 tablespoons soy sauce

2 tablespoons dry sherry

3 slices ginger, cut into ¼-inch-thick rounds

4 cloves garlic, smashed

12 whole chicken wings, cut in half at the joint, wingtip discarded (24 pieces total)

¾ cup sweet chili sauce

Sliced scallions for garnish (optional)

1. Add the stock, soy sauce, dry sherry, ginger, garlic, and wings to the inner pot. Stir to combine.

2. Lock the lid. Cook on high pressure for 10 minutes, then manually release the pressure.

3. Meanwhile, preheat the broiler. Transfer the wings to a baking sheet and broil them until crispy, about 3 to 5 minutes per side.

4. In a large bowl, add the chili sauce. Carefully transfer the broiled wings to the bowl, and toss to coat. Serve warm and garnished with scallions, if using.

HUMMUS

Sure, you can pick up packaged hummus from the grocery store or even make it from canned beans, but if those are the only two kinds of hummus you've had, you're in for a treat. The multi-cooker makes hummus from dried beans—which tastes far superior to hummus made from canned chickpeas—fast and accessible to just about everyone. The only ingredient you might not have on hand is tahini, which is sesame paste, but it's usually easy to find at the supermarket. Serve hummus as a dip with pita wedges, tortilla chips, or raw veggies, such as carrots and broccoli. **SERVES 4**

ACTIVE TIME: 10 minutes **PRESSURE TIME:** 15 minutes
RELEASE METHOD: Natural (15 minutes) **TOTAL TIME:** 50 minutes

---

1 cup chickpeas, soaked overnight

1 tablespoon extra-virgin olive oil, plus extra for serving

Kosher salt

1 large clove garlic, minced

½ cup tahini, well stirred

3 tablespoons lemon juice, plus more as needed to taste

½ teaspoon cumin

¼ teaspoon paprika, for garnish

1. Drain and rinse the soaked chickpeas. Add them along with the olive oil, ½ teaspoon of salt, and 4 cups of water to the pot.

2. Lock the lid. Cook on high pressure for 15 minutes. Let the pressure release naturally for 15 minutes, then manually release any remaining pressure. Drain the chickpeas.

3. Transfer the chickpeas to the bowl of a food processor along with the garlic, tahini, lemon juice, cumin, and 1 teaspoon of salt. Process until very smooth, adding cold water through the lid in a steady stream until the desired consistency is reached.

4. To serve, drizzle generously with olive oil and sprinkle with paprika.

SUPER-FAST TIP: Soaking the beans only takes a minute of planning, but it will save you 25 minutes of pressure time. Forgot to soak the beans? That's okay—you can still make the recipe. Cook the chickpeas on high pressure for 40 minutes. You can also cook the chickpeas a day in advance and store them in the fridge with some of their cooking liquid. The next day, drain them and proceed with step 3.

TAKEOUT CHINESE SPARERIBS

Spareribs are a popular appetizer favorite at Chinese restaurants, but have you ever thought about making them at home? All you need to do is stir together a few ingredients, marinate the ribs, and throw them in the multi-cooker. A few minutes under the broiler will caramelize them to perfection. Serve these as a starter on a night when you're making a vegetable stir-fry. **SERVES 4**

ACTIVE TIME: 20 minutes **PRESSURE TIME:** 30 minutes
RELEASE METHOD: Manual **TOTAL TIME:** 60 minutes (plus marinating time)

1½ teaspoons five-spice powder

½ teaspoon garlic powder

½ teaspoon ground ginger

2½ pounds St. Louis–style pork spareribs, trimmed of membrane and divided into 1-rib segments

½ cup hoisin sauce

¼ tablespoons soy sauce

2 tablespoons ketchup

2 tablespoons dry sherry

1 cup water

SMART TIP: Many Chinese sparerib recipes call for red food dye to give the ribs their distinctive color. You can certainly add a few drops to the marinating mixture, but this version omits it as it doesn't add anything to the flavor.

1. In a small bowl, mix together the five-spice powder, garlic powder, and ground ginger. Rub this mixture into the ribs and transfer them to a zip-top bag.

2. In a separate small bowl, stir together the hoisin, soy sauce, ketchup, and dry sherry. Add half of this sauce mixture to the zip-top bag, seal, and coat the ribs evenly. Reserve and refrigerate the remaining sauce for the glaze. Marinate the ribs in the refrigerator for at least an hour or as long as overnight.

3. When ready to cook, add 1 cup water to the inner pot before adding the ribs.

4. Lock the lid. Cook on high pressure for 30 minutes. Manually release the pressure.

5. Meanwhile, preheat the oven to broil, and line a sheet pan with foil. Transfer the ribs to the sheet pan and baste with some of the reserved sauce. Broil for 3 to 5 minutes, until caramelized. Flip, baste, and broil the ribs on the other side.

BUTTERNUT SQUASH SOUP

Creamy and subtly sweet, butternut squash soup is a fall and winter favorite. If you wish, in step 2, you can stir in 1 tablespoon of fresh ginger. **SERVES 4 TO 6**

ACTIVE TIME: 10 minutes **PRESSURE TIME:** 5 minutes
RELEASE: Natural (10 minutes) **TOTAL TIME:** 35 minutes

---

2 tablespoons unsalted butter

1 onion, chopped

6 cups peeled and cubed butternut squash

3 cups chicken or vegetable broth

2 teaspoons chopped fresh thyme leaves

1 pinch cayenne pepper

1 pinch ground nutmeg

Kosher salt

¼ cup heavy cream

1. Add the butter to the inner pot and heat on Sauté. Add the onion, and cook until translucent, about 3 minutes. Press Cancel to stop the cooking.

2. Add the squash, broth, thyme, cayenne, nutmeg, and ½ teaspoon of salt.

3. Lock the lid. Cook on high pressure for 5 minutes. Let the pressure release naturally for 10 minutes, then manually release any remaining pressure. The squash should easily break apart when pierced with a fork. Stir in the heavy cream.

4. Use an immersion blender to puree the soup or transfer it in batches to a blender to blend until smooth. Season to taste with additional salt if needed.

SUPER-FAST TIP: To get this soup on the table even faster, pick up pre-cut butternut squash at the supermarket.

COCONUT CARROT SOUP

Coconut Carrot Soup is incredibly frugal and surprisingly delicious. For a curried version, add 1 tablespoon of your favorite curry powder. **SERVES 4**

ACTIVE TIME: 10 minutes **PRESSURE TIME:** 2 minutes
RELEASE METHOD: Natural (10 minutes) **TOTAL TIME:** 25 minutes

---

1½ pounds carrots, peeled and thinly sliced

1 (13.5-ounce) can coconut milk

1 tablespoon minced fresh ginger

1 cup vegetable or chicken stock

1 tablespoon freshly squeezed lemon juice

1 tablespoon honey

Kosher salt and black pepper

Sliced scallions, for garnish (optional)

1. Add all of the ingredients to the inner pot and stir to combine.

2. Lock the lid. Cook on high pressure for 2 minutes. Let the pressure release naturally for 10 minutes, then manually release any remaining pressure.

3. Using an immersion blender, puree the soup, or transfer it to a regular blender and puree in batches.

4. Serve garnished with sliced scallions (if using).

FRENCH LENTIL SOUP

An inexpensive yet deliciously satisfying meal, French Lentil Soup comes together in just a few minutes. It's a thick soup, almost like a stew, so it's main-course worthy. Green lentils tend to be tastier and hold their shape better than brown lentils, but you can use brown as well. Chicken stock gives a nice rounded flavor to the soup, but a vegetable stock will keep the dish vegetarian. Serve this soup with crusty bread and butter on a cold night. **SERVES 4 TO 6**

ACTIVE TIME: 10 minutes **PRESSURE TIME:** 15 minutes
RELEASE: Natural (10 minutes) **TOTAL TIME:** 45 minutes

3 tablespoons olive oil

1 large onion, chopped

1 carrot, peeled and chopped

1 rib celery, chopped

2 large cloves garlic, minced

1 (14.5-ounce) can diced tomatoes in juice

1 cup green lentils, picked over for debris and rinsed

2½ cups chicken stock

1 teaspoon dried thyme leaves

Kosher salt and black pepper

2–3 tablespoons chopped fresh parsley

1. Heat the olive oil in the inner pot on Sauté. Add the onion, carrot, and celery, and cook, stirring frequently, for 2 to 3 minutes. Add the garlic and cook until fragrant, about 30 seconds.

2. Stir in the tomatoes and their juices, lentils, stock, thyme, ½ teaspoon of salt, and ½ teaspoon of pepper. Press Cancel.

3. Lock the lid. Cook on high pressure for 15 minutes. Allow the pressure to release naturally for 10 minutes, then manually release any remaining pressure. Test the lentils for doneness, and stir in the parsley.

BLACK BEAN SOUP

Garnish this hearty black bean soup with sour cream and diced avocado. If you wish, you can add a half cup of cubed ham in the second step. **SERVES 4 TO 6**

ACTIVE TIME: 10 minutes **PRESSURE TIME:** 5 minutes
RELEASE METHOD: Natural (10 minutes) **TOTAL TIME:** 35 minutes

---

2 tablespoons olive oil

1 chopped onion

2 cubanelle peppers (or 1 red bell pepper), seeded and chopped

1 rib celery, minced

3 cloves garlic, chopped

1 (29-ounce) can black beans, drained and rinsed

3 cups vegetable or chicken stock

1 teaspoon dried oregano

½ teaspoon garlic powder

½ teaspoon kosher salt

½ teaspoon freshly ground black pepper

4 tablespoons chopped fresh cilantro, divided

1. Heat the oil in the inner pot on Sauté. Add the onion, cubanelle peppers, celery, and garlic, and cook, stirring occasionally, for 5 minutes. Press Cancel to stop the cooking.

2. Add the beans, stock, oregano, garlic powder, salt, pepper, and 2 tablespoons cilantro to the pot. Stir to combine.

3. Lock the lid. Cook on high pressure for 5 minutes. Let the pressure release naturally for 10 minutes, then manually release any remaining pressure. Serve garnished with the remaining cilantro.

MANHATTAN CLAM CHOWDER

Unlike New England clam chowder, Manhattan Clam Chowder is tomato-based and a much better fit for the multi-cooker than a cream-based soup that would just split under pressure. **SERVES 4**

> **ACTIVE TIME:** 15 minutes **PRESSURE TIME:** 5 minutes
> **RELEASE METHOD:** Natural (5 minutes) **TOTAL TIME:** 35 minutes

1 teaspoon olive oil

3 slices bacon, chopped

1 large onion, chopped

1 rib celery, sliced

1 cubanelle pepper (or ½ green bell pepper), seeded and diced

1 clove garlic, minced

¾ pound red potatoes, cut into 1-inch pieces

1 (14-ounce) can diced tomatoes in juice

3 (8-ounce) bottles clam juice

2 (6-ounce) cans clams, drained and liquid reserved

½ teaspoon black pepper

1 bay leaf

1 teaspoon hot sauce, such as Tabasco (optional)

¼ cup chopped fresh parsley

Kosher salt, as needed

1. Heat the oil in the inner pot on Sauté. Add the bacon, and cook, stirring occasionally, until browned, 5 minutes. Stir in the onion, celery, and cubanelle pepper, and continue cooking until the onion is translucent, about 3 minutes. Stir in the garlic. Press Cancel to stop the cooking.

2. Add the potatoes, tomatoes and their juices, bottled clam juice, reserved clam juice from canned clams, black pepper, and hot sauce (if using).

3. Lock the lid. Cook on high pressure for 5 minutes. Let the pressure release naturally for 5 minutes, then manually release any remaining pressure. Stir in the clams and put the lid on top of the pot (do not lock it) until the clams are hot and cooked through. Stir in the parsley and taste to see if additional salt is needed; the clam juice is likely salty enough.

MINESTRONE SOUP

Wonderfully versatile, minestrone is a soup that allows you to use what you have on hand, making it as simple or complex as you want. If you happen to have a Parmesan rind left over after grating the cheese, toss it into the soup to infuse the broth with flavor. It's a great way of using up something that might otherwise be thrown away. **SERVES 4**

ACTIVE TIME: 10 minutes **PRESSURE TIME:** 5 minutes
RELEASE METHOD: Natural (10 minutes) **TOTAL TIME:** 35 minutes

---

1 zucchini, halved and cut into ¼-inch-thick slices

2 carrots, peeled and thinly sliced

1 onion, chopped

2 cups thinly sliced cabbage or kale

1 cup uncooked ditalini pasta or other small pasta (such as elbow macaroni)

1 (15.5-ounce) can cannellini or red kidney beans, drained and rinsed

1 (14-ounce) can diced tomatoes

3 cups vegetable or chicken stock

½ teaspoon kosher salt

½ teaspoon black pepper

¼ cup sliced fresh basil leaves, for garnish

Grated Parmesan cheese, for serving

Extra-virgin olive oil, for serving

1. Add the zucchini, carrot, onion, cabbage, pasta, beans, tomatoes, stock, salt, and pepper to the inner pot. The liquid should just cover the ingredients. If not, add a little water.

2. Cook on high pressure for 5 minutes. Let the pressure release naturally for 10 minutes then manually release any remaining pressure.

3. Serve garnished with basil, Parmesan cheese, and a drizzle of olive oil.

CHICKEN NOODLE SOUP

For a soup that's *almost* as easy as opening a can, try this Chicken Noodle Soup. You can even throw this together when you're feeling a little under the weather. **SERVES 4 TO 6**

ACTIVE TIME: 10 minutes **PRESSURE TIME:** 5 minutes
RELEASE METHOD: Natural (10 minutes) **TOTAL TIME:** 35 minutes

---

1 pound boneless skinless chicken thighs, cut into bite-sized pieces

½ teaspoon kosher salt

½ teaspoon black pepper

1 onion, chopped

1 large carrot, peeled and sliced into bite-sized pieces

1 russet potato, peeled and cut into bite-sized pieces

1 rib celery, thinly sliced

4 ounces egg noodles

2 tablespoons chopped fresh parsley, or 2 teaspoons dried parsley

4 to 5 cups chicken broth

½ cup frozen corn, thawed (optional)

1. Add all ingredients except the corn to the inner pot and stir to combine. The broth should just barely cover the ingredients, including the noodles. If it doesn't, add a bit more stock or water.

2. Lock the lid. Cook on high pressure for 5 minutes. Let the pressure release naturally for 10 minutes, then manually release any remaining pressure.

3. Stir in the corn (if using) and eat, preferably curled up under a warm blanket.

SMART TIP: Want to use leftover chicken? Tear the cooked meat into bite-sized pieces, and stir it in at the end with the corn, simmering for a few minutes to heat it though.

TORTILLA SOUP

If you love Mexican food, but have never tried tortilla soup, what are you waiting for? This version is simplified with the addition of flavor-packed jarred salsa. If you wish, you can crumble up tortilla chips in place of the sliced tortillas.

SERVES 4

> **ACTIVE TIME:** 15 minutes **PRESSURE TIME:** 5 minutes
> **RELEASE METHOD:** Natural (10 minutes) **TOTAL TIME:** 40 minutes

4 boneless, skinless chicken thighs, cut into bite-sized pieces

1 (15-ounce) can black beans, drained and rinsed

1 onion, chopped

1 carrot, peeled and chopped

1 cup jarred salsa (you choose the heat level)

2 cups chicken stock

½ teaspoon ground cumin

¼ teaspoon dried oregano

Kosher salt and black pepper

1 cup frozen corn, thawed (optional)

¼ cup chopped fresh cilantro

4 corn tortillas, sliced into bite-sized strips

Cubed avocado, for serving

Shredded cheddar cheese, for serving

1. Add the chicken, beans, onion, carrot, salsa, stock, cumin, oregano, ¼ teaspoon of salt, and ¼ teaspoon of pepper to the inner pot. Stir to combine.

2. Lock the lid and cook on high pressure for 5 minutes. Let the pressure release naturally for 10 minutes, then manually release any remaining pressure. Stir in the corn (if using) and cilantro.

3. Divide the soup among bowls, and top with strips of corn tortilla, avocado chunks, and cheese.

SAUCES AND PASTA

SUNDAY SAUCE

If you come from an Italian-American family, you're probably familiar with the concept of a Sunday Sauce. It's a slow-cooked meat sauce that simmers all morning on the stove and is ready in time for Sunday lunch. This recipe, however, takes under an hour! You can include various meats, but this version uses chicken wings and Italian sausage. (Sugar might seem like an unusual addition, but the small quantity helps to tame the acidity of the tomatoes.) Serve the sauce over pasta, and pass the meat separately at the table. **SERVES 6**

ACTIVE TIME: 15 minutes **PRESSURE TIME:** 10 minutes
RELEASE METHOD: Natural (10 minutes) **TOTAL TIME:** 45 minutes

---

2 tablespoons olive oil

1 onion, chopped

5 cloves garlic, thinly sliced

1 pinch red pepper flakes (or more to taste)

1 pound chicken wings, split and tips discarded or saved for stock

1 pound (about 4) hot or mild Italian sausage links, pricked with a fork

1 (28-ounce) can crushed tomatoes

1 (6-ounce) can tomato paste

1½ cups chicken stock or water

Kosher salt

1 teaspoon sugar

1 bay leaf (optional)

¼ cup lightly packed basil leaves, sliced

1½ pounds cooked pasta of your choice, for serving

Parmesan or Romano cheese, for serving

1. Heat the oil in the inner pot on Sauté. Add the onion and cook, stirring frequently, until translucent, about 3 minutes. Stir in the sliced garlic and cook until fragrant, about 30 seconds. Press Cancel to stop the cooking. Add a pinch of red pepper flakes.

2. Add the chicken wings, sausage, crushed tomatoes, tomato paste, stock, 1 teaspoon of salt, sugar, and bay leaf (if using). Stir to combine.

3. Lock the lid. Cook on high pressure for 10 minutes. Let the pressure release naturally for 10 minutes, then manually release any remaining pressure. The sausage should be cooked, and the meat on the chicken wings should start to separate from the bone when pierced with a fork.

4. Remove the bay leaf. Transfer the meat to a serving dish. If the sauce is too thin, simmer for a few minutes on Sauté to thicken. Stir in the basil.

5. Serve over cooked pasta, serving the meat and cheese at the table.

SUPER-FAST TIP: Put on a big pot of water to boil when you start cooking. You can always turn it down to simmer if it boils before you finish your prep work. Add the pasta to the water while the pot is depressurizing, and it will be ready when the sauce is.

MARINARA SAUCE

Marinara sauce is like the little black dress of the kitchen. It's incredibly versatile and goes with just about anything. That's why it's not a bad idea to make up a big batch and freeze it in smaller quantities for other uses. Try it in the Weeknight Pork Ragù (page 42), in the Baked Ziti (page 48), on pizza, or just over plain pasta. Plus, it's so much better than any jarred sauce out there! **SERVES 6 TO 8**

ACTIVE TIME: 15 minutes **PRESSURE TIME:** 10 minutes
RELEASE METHOD: Natural (10 minutes) **TOTAL TIME:** 45 minutes

---

¼ cup olive oil

1 onion, minced

5 cloves garlic, thinly sliced

1 cup dry red wine

2 (28-ounce) cans crushed tomatoes

2 tablespoons tomato paste

2 bay leaves

1 Parmesan cheese rind (optional)

Kosher salt

¼ teaspoon red pepper flakes

¼ cup thinly sliced fresh basil

Cooked pasta, for serving

Grated Parmesan or Romano cheese, for serving

1. Heat the oil in the inner pot on Sauté. Add the onion and garlic and cook, stirring frequently until the onions are translucent, about 3 minutes. Add the wine and simmer until the liquid is slightly reduced, about 2 minutes. Press Cancel to stop the cooking.

2. Add the tomatoes, tomato paste, bay leaves, Parmesan rind (if using), 2 teaspoons of salt, and the red pepper flakes.

3. Lock the lid. Cook on high pressure for 10 minutes. Let the pressure release naturally for 10 minutes, then manually release any remaining pressure. Taste and add more salt if needed. Remove the bay leaves and cheese rind (if used). Stir in the basil.

4. If the sauce is too thin, simmer it on Sauté until it reaches the desired consistency. Serve over cooked pasta with grated cheese.

SMART TIP: Sauce too tart? A pinch of sugar can help tame the acidity.

RIGATONI BOLOGNESE

Bolognese is a hearty meat sauce that's typically slow-cooked for hours on the stove—the longer the better. But who has time for that? This version is packed with flavor and takes just 10 minutes of pressure time. The multi-cooker makes Bolognese weeknight possible. **SERVES 4**

ACTIVE TIME: 15 minutes **PRESSURE TIME:** 10 minutes
RELEASE METHOD: Natural (5 minutes) **TOTAL TIME:** 45 minutes

---

2 tablespoons olive oil

1 onion, diced

1 rib celery, diced

1 carrot, peeled and diced

4 cloves garlic, minced

1 pound ground beef (or a mix of ground beef, pork, and veal)

1 cup beef or chicken stock

1 (14.5-ounce) can crushed tomatoes

1 bay leaf

Kosher salt and black pepper

¼ cup sliced basil leaves

1 pound cooked rigatoni (or your favorite pasta), for serving

Grated Parmesan cheese, for serving

1. Heat the oil in the inner pot on Sauté. Add the onion, celery, carrot, and garlic and cook, stirring occasionally, about 3 to 4 minutes.

2. Add the beef and cook, breaking up large chunks with a spoon, until browned. Add the stock and use the spoon to scrape up any browned bits on the bottom of the pot. Press Cancel to stop the cooking.

3. Stir in the tomatoes, bay leaf, 1½ teaspoons of salt, and ½ teaspoon of pepper.

4. Lock the lid. Cook on high pressure for 10 minutes. Let the pressure release naturally for 5 minutes, then manually release any remaining pressure. Remove the bay leaf, and stir in the basil.

5. Serve the sauce over the cooked pasta, and pass the Parmesan cheese around the table.

SMART TIP: Substitute up to ½ cup of the stock with red wine for a richer, more complex flavor.

WEEKNIGHT PORK RAGÙ

This is almost as easy as heating up a jar of tomato sauce—but infinitely tastier. After just 15 minutes of pressure time, the pork will be falling apart, cooked-all-day tender in the sauce. All you have to do is make a pot of pasta while the sauce cooks, and dinner is done. Don't forget the basil at the end; it adds a wonderful freshness to the dish. **SERVES 4**

ACTIVE TIME: 10 minutes **PRESSURE TIME:** 15 minutes
RELEASE METHOD: Natural (10 minutes) **TOTAL TIME:** 45 minutes

---

1 pound boneless pork shoulder, cut into 1-inch chunks

Kosher salt and black pepper

1 tablespoon olive oil

1 onion, chopped

3 cloves garlic, minced

1 (28-ounce) can crushed tomatoes

¼ cup coarsely chopped fresh basil leaves

1 pound cooked pasta, for serving

Grated Parmesan cheese, for serving

1. Season the pork with salt and pepper. Heat the oil in the inner pot on Sauté. Add the pork and sear until golden brown, about 2 to 3 minutes per side. Remove the pork from the pot, and set it aside.

2. Add the onion and garlic, and cook, stirring, for 2 to 3 minutes, scraping up any brown bits. Stir in the tomatoes and ½ teaspoon salt, and nestle the pork on top.

3. Lock the lid. Cook on high pressure for 15 minutes. Let the pressure release naturally for 10 minutes, then manually release any remaining pressure.

4. Shred the meat using two forks. Stir the meat into the sauce, along with the basil. Taste, and adjust the seasoning as needed. Serve over pasta and sprinkle with Parmesan.

SUPER-FAST TIP: If you're pressed for time, make this ragù with jarred tomato sauce. If your sauce is on the thicker side, add a little water so that it doesn't scorch under pressure. Skip the salt on the pork, sear it well, then add the sauce and proceed with the recipe.

PENNE WITH ITALIAN SAUSAGE, PEPPER, AND ONION

Inspired by the traditional Italian-American sausage and pepper sandwich, this tangy and spicy sauce is served over penne, but you're more than welcome to spoon it into crusty rolls. **SERVES 6**

ACTIVE TIME: 15 minutes **PRESSURE TIME:** 8 minutes
RELEASE METHOD: Natural (10 minutes) **TOTAL TIME:** 40 minutes

---

1 tablespoon olive oil

1 pound hot or mild Italian sausage, links pricked with a fork

1 red, yellow, or orange bell peppers, seeded and sliced

1 onion, peeled and sliced

1 jalapeño, seeded and thinly sliced (optional)

4 cloves garlic, minced

½ cup marsala or red wine

1 cup tomato sauce (such as Marinara Sauce, page 40)

¼ teaspoon dried oregano

¼ teaspoon dried basil

1 pound cooked penne pasta

Grated Parmesan cheese, for serving

1. Heat the oil in the inner pot on Sauté. Working in batches, brown the sausages well on all sides. Transfer browned sausages to a plate as you finish.

2. Add the bell pepper, onion, jalapeño (if using), and garlic to the pot and cook, stirring frequently until the onion is translucent, about 3 minutes. Stir in the wine, using a wooden spoon to help scrape up the brown bits. Press Cancel to stop the cooking.

3. Return the sausage and any accumulated juices to the pot along with the tomato sauce, oregano, and basil.

4. Lock the lid. Cook on high pressure for 8 minutes. Let the pressure release naturally for 10 minutes, then manually release any remaining pressure.

5. If the sauce is too thin, remove the sausages and simmer the sauce until it reaches the desired consistency. Serve over cooked pasta with Parmesan cheese.

FETTUCCINI WITH CHICKEN, SPINACH, AND ARTICHOKE SAUCE

Fettuccini is delicious with this creamy artichoke sauce, but another pasta shape will work just fine, including penne. **SERVES 4**

ACTIVE TIME: 15 minutes **PRESSURE TIME:** 8 minutes
RELEASE METHOD: Manual **TOTAL TIME:** 40 minutes

---

4 boneless, skinless chicken thighs

Kosher salt and black pepper

1 tablespoon olive oil

4 cloves garlic, minced

½ cup chicken stock

½ cup white wine

1 (14-ounce) jar artichoke hearts, drained and sliced

5 ounces baby spinach

½ cup heavy cream

½ cup grated Parmesan cheese, plus more for serving

2 tablespoons chopped fresh parsley

1 pound cooked fettuccini

Lemon wedges, for serving

1. Season the chicken with salt and pepper and set aside.

2. Heat the oil in the inner pot on Sauté. Add garlic and cook, stirring until fragrant, about 30 seconds. Press Cancel to stop the cooking.

3. Add the seasoned chicken, stock, and wine to the pot.

4. Lock the lid. Cook on high pressure for 8 minutes, then manually release the pressure. Remove the chicken to a plate to rest and tent with foil. When cool enough to handle, cut it into bite-sized pieces.

5. Set the pot to Sauté and reduce the sauce, stirring occasionally until it reaches the desired consistency, about 5 minutes. Return the chicken to the pot, along with the artichoke hearts, spinach, heavy cream, Parmesan, parsley, and fettuccini. Toss to coat. Place the lid back on the pot (do not lock it) to allow the spinach to wilt and the other ingredients to heat through. Season to taste with salt and pepper, and serve with more Parmesan and lemon wedges.

PASTA ALLA NORMA

Pasta alla Norma is a Sicilian eggplant and tomato sauce. It's usually served topped with grated ricotta salata, a hard, salty cheese, but this recipe calls for the much easier to find Romano cheese. By all means use the ricotta salata if your supermarket carries it, but to let you in on a secret, this dish is also great (though not so traditional) when topped with soft chunks of fresh mozzarella cheese that will get all melty and oozy. **SERVES 4**

ACTIVE TIME: 10 minutes   **PRESSURE TIME:** 5 minutes   **RELEASE METHOD:** Manual
TOTAL TIME: 25 minutes

---

2 tablespoons olive oil, plus more as needed

1 pound cubed eggplant

3 cloves garlic, minced

¼ teaspoon red pepper flakes

1 pint cherry tomatoes, halved

Kosher salt

½ cup lightly packed fresh basil leaves

1 pound cooked pasta (your choice)

Grated Romano cheese, for serving

1. Heat the oil in the inner pot on Sauté. Add the eggplant, and cook stirring occasionally until browned, about 5 minutes, adding extra oil if needed. Add the garlic and red pepper flakes and cook until fragrant, about 30 seconds. Stir in the cherry tomatoes and 1 teaspoon of salt.

2. Lock the lid. Cook on high pressure for 5 minutes, then manually release the pressure.

3. Meanwhile, thinly slice the basil. Stir the basil into the sauce and serve it over cooked pasta with Romano cheese.

SMART TIP: To save prep time, swap out the cherry tomatoes for 1 (28-ounce) can crushed tomatoes.

BAKED ZITI

This Baked Ziti is *almost* effortless. The pasta cooks directly in the sauce—infusing it with more flavor than you'd get just cooking it on the stove—and then is transferred to a baking dish, topped with cheese, and finished off under the broiler. For a pizza-inspired variation, omit the cream, and add sliced pepperoni to the top of the ziti along with the cheese. You could also toss in some cubed leftover sausage with the pasta in step 5. **SERVES 3 TO 4**

ACTIVE TIME: 10 minutes **PRESSURE TIME:** 5 minutes
RELEASE METHOD: Manual **TOTAL TIME:** 30 minutes

Nonstick cooking spray

2 tablespoons olive oil

3 cloves garlic, minced

12 ounces uncooked ziti

1 (24-ounce) jar your favorite tomato sauce or 3 cups Marinara Sauce (page 40)

1 cup water

½ cup heavy cream

¼ cup grated Parmesan cheese

4 ounces (about 1 cup) shredded mozzarella

1. Preheat the broiler, and spray an 8 x 8-inch baking pan with nonstick cooking spray.

2. Heat the oil in the inner pot on Sauté, and add the garlic. Cook, stirring frequently, until fragrant, about 30 seconds.

3. Add the pasta, sauce, and water, and stir to coat. The pasta should be mostly submerged in the sauce. If not, add a bit more water.

4. Lock the lid. Cook on low pressure for 5 minutes, then manually release the pressure (see Smart Tip). Stir in the heavy cream.

5. Transfer the pasta to the prepared dish. (If there's too much sauce, reserve extras to serve at the table.) Sprinkle the top evenly with the Parmesan and then the mozzarella cheese.

6. Transfer to the broiler and cook until the cheese is melted and golden brown in spots, 3 to 5 minutes.

PASTA E FAGIOLI

Somewhere between a soup and a stew lies Pasta e Fagioli, a beloved Italian pasta and bean dish with humble origins. This easy version is done in (almost) an instant. **SERVES 4 TO 6**

ACTIVE TIME: 10 minutes **PRESSURE TIME:** 5 minutes
RELEASE METHOD: Manual **TOTAL TIME:** 25 minutes

---

2 tablespoons extra-virgin olive oil, plus more for drizzling

1 onion, chopped

5 cloves garlic, minced

1 (29-ounce) can cannellini beans, drained and rinsed

1 (28-ounce) can diced tomatoes, drained

1 cup uncooked ditalini pasta

1 teaspoon oregano

1 bay leaf (optional)

Kosher salt and black pepper

3 cups chicken stock (more or less may be needed)

½ cup lightly packed, fresh basil leaves, sliced

Grated Parmesan cheese, for serving

1. Heat the oil in the inner pot on Sauté. Add the onion and garlic and cook, stirring frequently, until the onion is translucent, about 3 minutes. Press Cancel to stop the cooking.

2. Add the beans, tomatoes, pasta, oregano, bay leaf (if using), 1 teaspoon of salt, and ½ teaspoon of pepper, and stir to combine. Add enough stock to barely cover the ingredients, being careful not to overfill the pot. (It's okay if a few pasta pieces stick out.)

3. Lock the lid. Cook on high pressure for 5 minutes, then manually release the pressure. The pasta should be al dente (tender with just a little bit of bite). If needed, cook on simmer for a few minutes more until it reaches the desired doneness. Stir in the basil.

4. Serve with Parmesan cheese and a drizzle of olive oil.

SMART TIP: Pasta cooking times can vary slightly by multi-cooker, so it may take a bit of trial and error to find the right length of time for your model and your tastes. Start with 5 minutes on low. If the pasta is too firm for your taste, simmer on Sauté, adding more water if needed, until it reaches the desired doneness. If anything other than steam spits through the pressure release knob when you release the pressure, close it and wait a minute or two before trying again to avoid clogging it.

BEANS, GRAINS, AND CHILIS

HEARTY BEEF AND BEAN CHILI

This isn't humdrum ground beef chili. It's falling-apart-tender chunks of beef and dried beans from scratch in 15 minutes. (Okay, so you do have to soak the beans overnight, but this only requires a minute or two of planning.) Serve this dish with all your favorite chili toppings, such as crumbled tortilla or corn chips, diced onion, shredded cheese, cubed avocado, chopped jalapeño, chopped cilantro, lime wedges, or sour cream. **SERVES 6**

> **ACTIVE TIME:** 15 minutes **PRESSURE TIME:** 15 minutes
> **RELEASE METHOD:** Natural (10 minutes) **TOTAL TIME:** 50 minutes

1 tablespoon olive oil

1 onion, chopped

1 cubanelle or green bell pepper, chopped

3 cloves garlic, chopped

1½ pounds cubed chuck steak

Kosher salt and black pepper

½ pound pinto beans (or your favorite beans for chili), soaked overnight, drained, and rinsed

2 cups beef or chicken broth

2 tablespoons chili powder

1 teaspoon paprika

1 teaspoon cumin

1. Heat the oil in the inner pot on Sauté. Add the onion and cubanelle pepper, and cook until slightly softened, about 3 to 4 minutes. Stir in the garlic, and cook until just fragrant, about 30 seconds.

2. Season the chuck steak with salt and pepper, and add it to the pot. Cook until browned on all sides, about 5 minutes. Press Cancel to stop the cooking.

3. Add the beans, broth, chili powder, paprika, cumin, 1 teaspoon of salt, and ½ teaspoon of black pepper. The broth should cover the beans by about one inch. If it doesn't, add water to make up the difference.

4. Lock the lid. Cook on high pressure for 15 minutes. Allow the pressure to release naturally for 10 minutes, then manually release any remaining pressure.

5. Adjust seasoning if necessary, and simmer if desired to reduce the remaining liquid.

VEGGIE CHILI

Veggie Chili is packed with delicious goodness. The soy sauce may sound like a strange addition, but it gives a savory, rounded flavor in the absence of meat products. **SERVES 4 TO 6**

ACTIVE TIME: 15 minutes **PRESSURE TIME:** 5 minutes
RELEASE METHOD: Manual **TOTAL TIME:** 30 minutes

¼ cup olive oil

4 to 5 cloves garlic, thinly sliced

1 eggplant, cubed

1 zucchini, cubed

1 red bell pepper, seeded and chopped

1 carrot, peeled and chopped

1 onion, chopped

1 cup chopped mushrooms

1 (14-ounce) can diced tomatoes (preferably fire roasted)

1 (14.5-ounce) can black or kidney beans, drained and rinsed

1 cup vegetable broth

1 tablespoon soy sauce

1 tablespoon tomato paste

2 tablespoons chili powder

1 teaspoon dried oregano

1 teaspoon ground cumin

1 teaspoon salt

1. Heat the oil in the inner pot on Sauté. Add the garlic and stir until fragrant, about 30 seconds. Press Cancel to stop the cooking.

2. Add the remaining ingredients to the pot.

3. Lock the lid. Cook on high pressure for 5 minutes, then manually release the pressure.

4. Serve with your favorite chili toppings, such as cheese, sour cream, diced onions, and sliced avocado.

TACO CHILI

Taco chili is simply a regular chili that's been flavored with the same seasonings you'd use in tacos. That means a lot fewer spices to measure! Serve with any and all of your favorite taco or chili toppings. You can even use this chili as a base for layered nachos. The tomatoes are added at the end so that their acidity doesn't stop the beans from cooking evenly. **SERVES 6**

ACTIVE TIME: 15 minutes **PRESSURE TIME:** 10 minutes
RELEASE METHOD: Natural (15 minutes) **TOTAL TIME:** 45 minutes

---

2 tablespoons olive oil

1 onion, chopped

5 cloves garlic, minced

1 pound ground beef

1 cup dried black beans, soaked overnight

1 cup dried pinto beans, soaked overnight

4 tablespoons taco seasoning mix

1 tablespoon chili powder

2 teaspoons cumin

½ teaspoon freshly ground black pepper

1 (4-ounce) can diced green chiles

1 (14.5-ounce) can diced tomatoes, drained

1. Heat the oil in the inner pot on Sauté. Add the onion and garlic, and cook, stirring occasionally until the onion is translucent, about 3 minutes. Add the beef and cook, breaking up large chunks with a wooden spoon.

2. Drain and rinse the beans, and add them to the pot, along with the taco seasoning mix, chili powder, cumin, black pepper, green chiles, and water to cover the ingredients by about one inch.

3. Lock the lid. Cook on high pressure for 10 minutes. Allow the pressure to release naturally for 15 minutes, then manually release any remaining pressure.

4. Stir in the tomatoes and simmer for a few minutes on Sauté to allow the flavors to blend. Taste and add additional salt and pepper if needed.

SUPER-FAST TIP: By soaking the beans overnight, you reduce the required pressure time by 10 to 12 minutes, so that you can get dinner on the table faster.

TURKEY, BLACK BEAN, AND SWEET POTATO CHILI

Smoky, savory, and sweet, this chili checks all the right boxes. You can substitute ground beef for the ground turkey if that's what you have on hand. **SERVES 4 TO 6**

> **ACTIVE TIME:** 10 minutes **PRESSURE TIME:** 10 minutes
> **RELEASE METHOD:** Manual **TOTAL TIME:** 30 minutes

2 tablespoons olive oil

1 pound ground turkey (preferably from dark meat)

Kosher salt and black pepper

1 large onion, chopped

3 cloves garlic, minced

1 sweet potato (about 1 pound), peeled and cut into 1-inch chunks

1 (15.5-ounce) can black beans, drained and rinsed

1 (10-ounce) can diced tomatoes and green chiles

1 cup chicken stock or water

½ chipotle chile in adobo, minced

½ teaspoon cumin

½ teaspoon oregano

½ teaspoon paprika

1 tablespoon honey

Shredded cheddar cheese, for serving

Sour cream, for serving

1. Heat the oil in the inner pot on Sauté. Add the turkey and cook, breaking up large chunks with a wooden spoon, about 5 minutes. Season with salt and pepper. Add the onion and garlic and stir until the garlic is fragrant, about 30 seconds. Press Cancel to stop the cooking.

2. Add the sweet potato, black beans, tomatoes, stock, chipotle, cumin, oregano, paprika, and honey. Stir to combine.

3. Cook on high pressure for 10 minutes, then manually release the pressure. The sweet potato should be tender when pierced with a fork. If it's still firm, cook for a few minutes on Sauté. Add more salt and pepper to taste if needed. Serve with cheddar cheese and sour cream for topping.

ZUCCHINI AND PEA RISOTTO

Don't try to add too much to this delicate yet comforting risotto. The key is simplicity. **SERVES 4**

> **ACTIVE TIME:** 10 minutes **PRESSURE TIME:** 6 minutes
> **RELEASE METHOD:** Manual **TOTAL TIME:** 35 minutes

3 tablespoons unsalted butter, divided

1 small onion, chopped

1½ cups Arborio rice

2 medium zucchini, halved lengthwise and thinly sliced

½ cup dry white wine

3 cups vegetable broth, plus more if needed

Kosher salt and black pepper

½ cup grated Parmesan or Romano cheese

1 cup frozen peas, thawed

1. Heat 2 tablespoons of the butter in the inner pot on Sauté. After the butter melts and the foam subsides, add the onion and cook until translucent, about 3 minutes.

2. Add the rice and stir until coated and translucent, about 1 to 2 minutes. Add the zucchini, wine, broth, ¼ teaspoon of salt, and ¼ teaspoon of pepper, and stir until combined.

3. Lock the lid. Cook on high pressure for 6 minutes, then manually release the pressure.

4. Test the rice. It should be tender but with a little bite. If it needs more time, cook on Sauté, adding more stock as needed, until tender.

5. Stir in the Parmesan, peas, and remaining 1 tablespoon of butter and allow to heat through a few minutes before serving. The rice will thicken as it cools.

CHEESY ROTISSERIE CHICKEN RISOTTO

Cheesy Rotisserie Chicken Risotto takes two simple things—short-grain Arborio rice and leftover chicken—and transforms them into something extraordinarily comforting. Forget stirring and stirring at the stove with one pot of steaming rice and one pot of steaming broth. Once you lock the lid, your job is done! So, go ahead and pour yourself a glass of wine while you wait. **SERVES 4**

ACTIVE TIME: 10 minutes **PRESSURE TIME:** 6 minutes **RELEASE METHOD:** Manual
TOTAL TIME: 35 minutes

4 tablespoons unsalted butter

1 small onion, finely chopped

1½ cups Arborio rice

½ cup white wine

Kosher salt and black pepper

3½ cups chicken stock, plus more as needed

½ pound leftover cooked chicken, torn into bite-sized pieces

1 cup frozen peas, thawed

½ cup shredded fontina or Gouda cheese

¼ cup grated Parmesan cheese

2 to 3 tablespoons chopped fresh parsley or scallions

1. Heat the butter in the inner pot on Sauté. After the butter melts and the foam subsides, add the onion and cook until translucent, about 3 minutes.

2. Add the rice and stir until coated and translucent, about 1 to 2 minutes. Stir in the wine, ½ teaspoon of salt, and ½ teaspoon of pepper, and cook until the wine is almost evaporated, about 3 to 4 minutes. Press Cancel to stop the cooking. Stir in the chicken stock.

3. Lock the lid. Cook on high pressure for 8 minutes, then manually release the pressure.

4. Test the rice. It should be tender but with a little bite. If it needs more time, cook on Sauté, adding more stock as needed, until tender.

5. Stir in the chicken, peas, and both cheeses. Place the lid back on the multi-cooker (do not lock it), and let it set for 5 minutes, or until the cheese is melted and the chicken is heated through. Add more salt and pepper if needed, and stir in the parsley.

VEGETABLE THAI GREEN CURRY

Thai curry paste comes in a small jar and is a wonderful thing to have in the refrigerator whenever the craving for Thai food strikes. This healthy and delicious curry is faster and better than takeout. **SERVES 4**

ACTIVE TIME: 10 minutes **PRESSURE TIME:** 8 minutes
RELEASE METHOD: Manual **TOTAL TIME:** 25 minutes

1 large sweet potato, peeled and cut into 1-inch chunks

2 Chinese eggplants (or 1 regular eggplant), cut into 1-inch chunks

1 (14-ounce) package extra-firm tofu, drained and cut into 1-inch chunks

1 red bell pepper, seeded and sliced

1 onion, thinly sliced

1 cup coconut milk

¼ cup vegetable stock

2 tablespoons Thai green curry paste (or more to taste)

2 tablespoons soy sauce (or fish sauce if you're not vegetarian)

2 tablespoons packed brown sugar

½ cup lightly packed basil (preferably Thai basil), thinly sliced

Cooked jasmine rice, for serving

Lime wedges, for serving

1. Add the sweet potato, eggplant, tofu, pepper, onion, coconut milk, stock, curry paste, soy sauce, and brown sugar to the multi-cooker. Stir to combine.

2. Lock the lid. Cook on high pressure for 8 minutes, then manually release the pressure. The sweet potato should be tender when pierced with a fork. If not, simmer it for a few extra minutes until tender. Stir in the basil.

3. Serve over jasmine rice with a side of lime wedges.

SPICED INDIAN RED LENTILS

Red lentils are quite different than their brown, green, and black cousins. They practically dissolve when cooked, making a deliciously thick stew. Serve Spiced Indian Red Lentils over basmati rice, or scoop them up with warmed naan, which you can pick up from your favorite Indian restaurant or prepackaged from the supermarket. You could even eat this as a soup if you wish. **SERVES 4**

ACTIVE TIME: 10 minutes **PRESSURE TIME:** 10 minutes
RELEASE METHOD: Natural (10 minutes) **TOTAL TIME:** 40 minutes

---

2 tablespoons canola or peanut oil

1 red onion, chopped

1 tablespoon minced garlic

1 tablespoon minced ginger

1 jalapeño pepper, seeded and chopped (optional)

½ teaspoon whole cumin seeds

1 teaspoon turmeric

1 tablespoon garam masala, or your favorite curry powder

1 cup red lentils, picked over for debris and stones and well rinsed

Kosher salt

½ cup diced tomatoes (fresh or canned)

2 cups vegetable stock

2 tablespoons chopped fresh cilantro leaves

Plain yogurt, for serving

Lime wedges, for serving

1. Heat the oil in the inner pot on Sauté. Add the onion, and cook, stirring occasionally until translucent, about 3 minutes. Stir in the garlic, ginger, and jalapeño (if using) and cook until fragrant, about 30 seconds. Press Cancel to stop the cooking. Add the spices, and stir to coat and bloom them. (See Smart Tip.)

2. Add the lentils, 1 teaspoon of salt, tomatoes, and stock to the pot. Stir to combine.

3. Lock the lid. Cook on high pressure for 10 minutes. Let the pressure release naturally for 10 minutes, then manually release any remaining pressure. Stir in the cilantro.

4. Serve this dish with yogurt to dollop on top and lime wedges for a squeeze of citrus.

SMART TIP: Cooking the spices in the hot oil (a process called "blooming") helps release their flavor and fragrance. There's enough residual heat to do so after you press Cancel.

SHRIMP AND GRITS

This dish is a Southern classic. Grits can usually take 45 minutes to an hour to cook, but this version cooks in 15 minutes of pressure time, and no stirring is needed! You can also make the grits as a side dish without the shrimp. **SERVES 4 TO 6**

> **ACTIVE TIME:** 20 minutes **PRESSURE TIME:** 15 minutes
> **RELEASE METHOD:** Natural (15 minutes) **TOTAL TIME:** 60 minutes

Nonstick cooking spray

1 cup coarse-ground grits

3 cups water

3 tablespoons unsalted butter (2 tablespoons melted)

¾ teaspoon kosher salt, divided

2 ounces (about ¼ cup) shredded sharp cheddar cheese

2 ounces (about ¼ cup) shredded Monterey Jack cheese

2 tablespoons grated Parmesan cheese

4 slices bacon, chopped

4 scallions, light and green parts divided, thinly sliced

1½ pounds peeled and deveined shrimp

½ cup chicken stock

1 teaspoon hot sauce, plus more for serving

1 tablespoon freshly squeezed lemon juice

1. Add 2 cups of water to the inner pot. Insert the steam rack. Spray a high-sided 7-inch round baking pan or soufflé dish with cooking spray.

2. Add the grits, 3 cups of water, melted butter, and ½ teaspoon of the salt to the baking pan, and stir to combine.

3. Using a foil sling (see page 11), lower the pan, uncovered, into the inner pot, tucking in the ends.

4. Lock the lid. Cook on high pressure for 15 minutes. Let the pressure release naturally for 15 minutes, then manually release any remaining pressure. Stir in the cheeses to melt.

5. Meanwhile, add the bacon to a large skillet, and cook over medium heat until golden brown, about 5 to 7 minutes. Transfer the bacon to a paper towel–lined plate to drain.

6. Add the light green scallion parts to the skillet, and sauté briefly. Add the shrimp in a single layer and sear for 1 to 2 minutes per side.

7. Stir in the chicken stock, hot sauce, and remaining ¼ teaspoon of salt, using a wooden spoon to loosen up the brown bits. Cook until slightly reduced, about 1 minute. Remove immediately from the heat and add the lemon juice and butter, stirring until the butter is melted. Taste the sauce and add salt if needed.

8. Serve the shrimp and sauce over the grits, and garnish with the scallion greens.

SUPER-FAST TIP: While the grits are cooking, prepare your remaining ingredients. When the pressure time is almost up, start making the shrimp, so that they'll be ready by the end of the release period.

JAMBALAYA

Jambalaya, a Louisiana meat, seafood, and rice staple, is quick and easy in the multi-cooker. By browning the sausage first and then stirring it in only at the end, you infuse the rice with its flavor, yet keep it from turning rubbery under pressure. **SERVES 4**

ACTIVE TIME: 15 minutes **PRESSURE TIME:** 6 minutes
RELEASE METHOD: Manual **TOTAL TIME:** 35 minutes

2 tablespoons olive oil

8 ounces andouille sausage, cut into ¼-inch-thick slices

1 onion, chopped

1 green bell pepper, seeded and chopped

1 rib celery, chopped

3 cloves garlic, minced

2 teaspoons Cajun seasoning

¼ teaspoon ground thyme

1 cup long-grain rice

1 (14-ounce) can diced tomatoes

1½ cups chicken stock

Kosher salt

½ pound cooked shrimp

4 scallions, thinly sliced

1. Heat the olive oil in the inner pot at on Sauté. Add the sausage slices, and cook until browned, about 2 minutes per side. Transfer the meat to a paper towel–lined plate to drain.

2. Add the onion, bell pepper, celery, and garlic and cook, stirring occasionally, until the onion is translucent, about 3 minutes. Add the Cajun seasoning, thyme, and rice, and stir until the rice is well coated in the oil. Press Cancel to stop the cooking.

3. Add the tomatoes and their juices, the stock, and ½ teaspoon of salt. Stir.

4. Lock the lid. Cook on high pressure for 6 minutes, then manually release the pressure.

5. Stir in the shrimp, scallions, and reserved sausage. Allow the ingredients to heat through for a few minutes before serving.

CAULIFLOWER AND POTATO CURRY

Cauliflower and potato may each be relatively mild on their own, but they're packed with flavor when combined with spicy (but not hot!) curry powder. This dish is hearty, healthy, and delicious. **SERVES 4**

ACTIVE TIME: 10 minutes **PRESSURE TIME:** 5 minutes
RELEASE METHOD: Manual **TOTAL TIME:** 25 minutes

---

2 tablespoons unsalted butter or canola oil

1 onion, chopped

1 tablespoon minced garlic

1 tablespoon minced ginger

2 tablespoons mild curry powder

1 teaspoon cumin seeds

1 head cauliflower, cored and cut into bite-sized florets

1 pound red potatoes, cut into 1-inch chunks

2 plum tomatoes, seeded and chopped

1¼ cups vegetable stock

Kosher salt

2 tablespoons freshly chopped cilantro

Plain yogurt for serving (optional)

1. Add the butter to the pan and melt on Sauté. Add the onions and cook, stirring frequently until translucent, about 3 minutes. Add the garlic, ginger, curry powder, and cumin seeds, and cook until fragrant, about 30 seconds. Press Cancel.

2. Add the cauliflower, potatoes, tomatoes, stock, and ½ teaspoon of salt, and stir to combine.

3. Lock the lid. Cook on high pressure for 5 minutes. Manually release the pressure.

4. Stir in the cilantro, and serve over basmati rice with dollops of yogurt (if using).

VEGETARIAN RED BEANS AND RICE

Traditionally made on a Monday—which was wash day—red beans and rice is a slow-cooked dish that often takes hours to make. Most of the cooking is hands-off, which makes it a great match for a speedy pressure-cooker version. Ten minutes under pressure is all it takes. While it cooks, make a big pot of rice to serve with it. If you wish, you can also fry up some veggie andouille sausage.

SERVES 4

ACTIVE TIME: 10 minutes PRESSURE TIME: 10 minutes
RELEASE METHOD: Natural (15 minutes) TOTAL TIME: 45 minutes

1 tablespoon olive oil

1 green bell pepper, seeded and diced

1 large onion, chopped

2 ribs celery, thinly sliced

5 cloves garlic, minced

2 teaspoons Cajun seasoning

¼ teaspoon ground thyme

½ teaspoon ground oregano

½ pound small red beans, soaked overnight

3 cups vegetable stock

Kosher salt

¼ cup chopped fresh parsley

Cooked rice, for serving

Hot sauce, for serving

1. Heat the oil in the inner pot on Sauté. Add the pepper, onion, celery, and garlic, and cook, stirring frequently until the onion is translucent, about 3 minutes. Press Cancel to stop the cooking. Add the Cajun seasoning, thyme, and oregano, and stir to coat the vegetables evenly.

2. Drain and rinse the soaked beans, and add them to the pot along with the stock and salt to taste.

3. Lock the lid. Cook on high pressure for 10 minutes. Let the pressure release naturally for 15 minutes, then manually release any remaining pressure. Test the beans for doneness. If they are still too firm, return them to high pressure for a few minutes.

4. Stir in the parsley, and serve over rice with hot sauce on the side.

CHICKEN
AND TURKEY

MUSTARD TARRAGON CHICKEN

Practically a pantry dish, Mustard Tarragon Chicken gives you a little ooh-la-la in the middle of the work week. Serve over buttered egg noodles with extra sauce. **SERVES 4**

ACTIVE TIME: 10 minutes **PRESSURE TIME:** 10 minutes
RELEASE: Manual **TOTAL TIME:** 30 minutes

---

6 bone-in chicken thighs (about 2½ pounds), skin removed

Kosher salt and black pepper

2 teaspoons neutral-flavored oil, such as canola, vegetable, or grapeseed

3 to 4 cloves garlic, crushed

2 carrots, peeled and chopped

3 Yukon gold potatoes, cut into 1-inch cubes

2 sprigs tarragon, roughly torn

½ cup dry white wine

½ cup chicken stock

2 tablespoons Dijon mustard

2 tablespoons heavy cream

1. Season the chicken with salt and pepper, and set it aside.

2. Heat the oil in the inner pot on Sauté. Add the garlic, and cook and stir until lightly golden. Press Cancel to stop the cooking.

3. Add the carrot, potato, tarragon, white wine, chicken stock, mustard, and reserved chicken thighs.

4. Lock the lid. Cook on high pressure for 10 minutes, then manually release the pressure.

5. Carefully remove the lid and stir in the heavy cream.

SMART TIP: If there's too much liquid in the pot at the end of the cooking process, you can simmer it to reduce it or thicken it with 1 tablespoon of cornstarch dissolved in a little bit of water. Switch the machine to Sauté, and stir in the mixture until it thickens, about 1 minute. Then stir in the heavy cream.

PAPRIKA CHICKEN

Paprika Chicken is a favorite dish that's even more delicious served with buttered noodles and dollops of sour cream. Use real Hungarian paprika if you can find it; it often comes in a tin container in the spice aisle. Hint: If you can't remember how old your paprika is, it's better to use a fresh jar because it makes all of the difference in the flavor of this dish. **SERVES 4**

ACTIVE TIME: 10 minutes **PRESSURE TIME:** 10 minutes
RELEASE METHOD: Manual **TOTAL TIME:** 35 minutes

6 bone-in chicken thighs (about 2½ pounds), skin removed

Kosher salt and ground pepper

1 tablespoon olive oil

1 onion, chopped

1 cubanelle or red bell pepper, seeded and chopped

2 tablespoons sweet paprika

½ cup canned pureed tomatoes

½ cup chicken stock

½ teaspoon salt

Sour cream, for serving

Chopped fresh chives, for garnish (optional)

1. Season the chicken with salt and pepper, and set it aside.

2. Heat the oil in the inner pot on Sauté. Stir in the onion and cubanelle pepper, and cook, stirring occasionally, about 3 to 4 minutes. Press Cancel to stop the cooking. Add the paprika and stir to bloom the spice, about 1 minute.

3. Add the seasoned chicken to the pot along with the tomatoes, stock, and ½ teaspoon of salt.

4. Lock the lid. Cook on high pressure for 10 minutes, then manually release the pressure.

5. Serve with dollops of sour cream and chives (if using).

SMART TIP: You can substitute boneless chicken thighs in this recipe. Just decrease the pressure time to 8 minutes.

MANGO CHICKEN CURRY IN A HURRY

Though the ingredients list here is relatively conventional, this chicken curry is surprisingly delicious thanks to the addition of coconut milk and fresh mango. Maximum flavor for minimum effort, you might say! Serve Mango Chicken Curry over rice—basmati would be perfect—and a salad for a complete meal. **SERVES 4**

ACTIVE TIME: 10 minutes **PRESSURE TIME:** 8 minutes
RELEASE METHOD: Manual **TOTAL TIME:** 30 minutes

6 boneless, skinless chicken thighs

Kosher salt and black pepper

1 tablespoon olive oil

1 large yellow onion, chopped

2 to 3 cloves garlic, minced

2 tablespoons curry powder

1 (14.5-ounce) can diced tomatoes, drained

1 cup coconut milk

1 ripe mango, peeled and cubed

2 tablespoons chopped fresh cilantro

1. Season the chicken with salt and pepper, and set it aside.

2. Heat the oil in the inner pot on Sauté. Add the onion and cook, stirring frequently until just starting to brown on the edges, about 4 to 5 minutes. Stir in the garlic and cook until fragrant, about 30 seconds. Press Cancel to stop the cooking. Stir in the curry powder to bloom it and coat the onion mixture.

3. Add the seasoned chicken, canned tomatoes, coconut milk, and ½ teaspoon of salt to the pot.

4. Lock the lid. Cook on high pressure for 8 minutes, then manually release the pressure. Stir in the mango and cilantro.

CHICKEN PARMESAN

This delicate and healthier Chicken Parmesan is cooked in tomato sauce (not breaded and fried in oil!) and then topped with two kinds of cheese. Serve over your favorite pasta, which you can cook while the multi-cooker is taking care of the rest. **SERVES 4**

ACTIVE TIME: 5 minutes **PRESSURE TIME:** 8 minutes
RELEASE METHOD: Manual **TOTAL TIME:** 35 minutes

---

4 boneless, skinless chicken breasts

Kosher salt and black pepper

1 (24-ounce) jar tomato sauce or 3 cups Marinara Sauce (page 40)

¼ cup thinly sliced fresh basil, divided

4 ounces (about 1 cup) shredded mozzarella cheese

¼ cup grated Parmesan cheese, plus more for serving

1 pound cooked pasta, for serving

1. Season the chicken lightly with salt and pepper. Add the sauce to the multi-cooker and place the seasoned chicken on top. Spoon a little bit of sauce on top of the chicken to cover it.

2. Lock the lid. Cook on high pressure for 8 minutes, then manually release the pressure.

3. Carefully open the lid and stir in half of the fresh basil. Top the chicken evenly with the mozzarella, then the Parmesan. Set the lid back on top to let the cheese melt (about 5 minutes), but do not lock it.

4. Serve the chicken over cooked pasta and garnish with the remaining basil. Serve with additional Parmesan (if using).

CHICKEN WITH LEMON AND CAPER SAUCE

Also known as *chicken piccata*, Chicken with Lemon and Caper Sauce is tangy and savory. If you love capers, go for the full 3 tablespoons! **SERVES 4**

ACTIVE TIME: 15 minutes **PRESSURE TIME:** 8 minutes
RELEASE METHOD: Manual **TOTAL TIME:** 35 minutes

---

4 boneless, skinless chicken breasts

Kosher salt and black pepper

2 tablespoons olive oil

2 cloves garlic, minced

1 cup chicken stock

2–3 tablespoons drained capers

3 tablespoons unsalted butter, cut into slices

Juice of 1 lemon

1. Season the chicken with salt and pepper. Heat the oil in the inner pot on Sauté. Working with two chicken breasts at a time, brown the chicken, about 2 minutes per side. Add the garlic and cook until fragrant, about 30 seconds.

2. Add the stock to the pot along with the reserved chicken.

3. Lock the lid. Cook on high pressure for 8 minutes, then manually release the pressure.

4. Transfer the chicken to a plate to rest, and tent the meat with foil.

5. Heat the remaining sauce on Sauté until it thickens to the desired consistency, about 5 minutes. Press Cancel. Add the sliced butter and lemon, and stir until the butter is melted. Taste and add any additional salt and pepper needed.

6. Return the chicken along with any accumulated juices to the pot to coat the chicken. Serve with the sauce.

MEDITERRANEAN CHICKEN WITH OLIVES

Mediterranean Chicken with Olives adds a salty and briny kick to your chicken routine. Even if you don't think you like anchovies, give them a shot in this dish. You won't be able to pick out their flavor, but they'll give a nice umami boost to the dish. **SERVES 4**

ACTIVE TIME: 10 minutes **PRESSURE TIME:** 10 minutes
RELEASE METHOD: Manual **TOTAL TIME:** 30 minutes

---

6 bone-in chicken thighs (about 3 pounds), skin removed

Kosher salt and black pepper

1 tablespoon olive oil

1 red, yellow, or orange bell pepper, seeded and chopped

1 onion, chopped

1 small head garlic, sliced in half

2 anchovies, chopped (optional)

2 plum tomatoes, seeded and chopped

½ teaspoon dried marjoram or oregano

½ cup pitted black olives, such as Kalamata

1 cup chicken stock

1 tablespoon lemon juice

2 tablespoons chopped fresh parsley, for garnish

1. Season the chicken with salt and pepper, and set it aside.

2. Heat the oil in the inner pot on Sauté. Add the bell pepper, onion, and garlic, and cook, stirring frequently until the onion is translucent, about 3 minutes. Stir in the anchovies (if using), and cook until broken up and mostly dissolved, about another minute. Press Cancel to stop the cooking.

3. Add the seasoned chicken, tomatoes, marjoram, olives, stock, and ½ teaspoon of salt. Stir to combine.

4. Lock the lid. Cook on high pressure for 10 minutes, then manually release the pressure.

5. Stir in the lemon juice and parsley.

CHICKEN AND CHICKPEA TAGINE

A tagine is a North African stew, and the word *tagine* refers to the unique clay or ceramic vessel that is traditionally used to make it. Except for the optional saffron, there's nothing particularly fancy about the ingredients in this Chicken and Chickpea Tagine, but when you combine them all together they make quite the sophisticated and impressive dish. Streamline the prep by mixing together your dry spices first in a small bowl and setting them aside until needed. **SERVES 6**

ACTIVE TIME: 10 minutes **PRESSURE TIME:** 8 minutes
RELEASE METHOD: Manual **TOTAL TIME:** 30 minutes

---

6 boneless, skin-on chicken thighs and/or drumsticks (about 2½ pounds)

Kosher salt

2 tablespoons olive oil

2 carrots, peeled and sliced

3 shallots, finely chopped

3 cloves garlic, minced

1 teaspoon coriander

1 teaspoon ginger

1 teaspoon cumin

1 teaspoon paprika

½ teaspoon cinnamon

1 pinch saffron (optional)

1 (15.5-ounce) can chickpeas, drained and rinsed

1½ cups chicken stock

1 tablespoon tomato paste

1 tablespoon honey

2 tablespoons lemon juice

2 tablespoons minced fresh cilantro

2 tablespoons minced fresh parsley

Cooked couscous, for serving

1. Season the chicken with salt, and set it aside.

2. Heat the oil in the inner pot on Sauté. Add the carrots and shallots, and cook, stirring occasionally until the shallots are translucent, 2 to 3 minutes. Stir in the garlic and cook until fragrant, about 30 seconds. Press Cancel to stop the cooking. Stir in the spices (see Smart Tip page 61).

3. Add the seasoned chicken, chickpeas, stock, tomato paste, honey, and 1 teaspoon of salt.

4. Lock the lid. Cook on high pressure for 8 minutes, then manually release the pressure.

5. If there is too much liquid, simmer for a few minutes on Sauté to reduce to the desired consistency. Stir in the lemon juice, cilantro, and parsley. Serve over cooked couscous.

QUICK AND EASY TERIYAKI CHICKEN

This teriyaki chicken dish couldn't be simpler. Just mix together soy sauce and mirin, add some garlic and ginger, and you're off! If you're unfamiliar with mirin, it's a sweet Japanese rice wine and is usually found with the Asian food in the grocery store. You may also find it at the health food store or an Asian market. Once you realize how easy it is to make teriyaki sauce yourself, you may never go back to the bottled version again! **SERVES 4 TO 6**

ACTIVE TIME: 5 minutes **PRESSURE TIME:** 8 minutes
RELEASE METHOD: Natural (5 minutes) **TOTAL TIME:** 30 minutes

½ cup soy sauce

½ cup mirin

1 tablespoon minced garlic

1 tablespoon minced ginger

8 boneless, skinless chicken thighs (about 2½ pounds)

4 scallions (green parts only), thinly sliced

Sesame seeds, for garnish

1. Add the soy sauce, mirin, ginger, and garlic to the pot and stir to combine.

2. Lock the lid. Cook on high pressure for 8 minutes. Let the pressure release naturally for 5 minutes, then manually release the remaining pressure.

3. If desired, remove the chicken and cook the teriyaki sauce a few minutes on Sauté to thicken it into a glaze. Drizzle the chicken with a little extra sauce, and sprinkle the top with scallions and sesame seeds. Serve with rice.

SMART TIP: Since this dish has so few ingredients, quality is important. Use a high-quality soy sauce, one without additives, such as caramel color or corn syrup. It will make a big difference in the flavor.

PUERTO RICAN CHICKEN STEW

Pollo guisado means "stewed chicken" in Spanish, and this typical Puerto Rican stew is comfort food at its finest. Leftovers taste even better the next day. Many people add Sazón seasoning packets (find them in the spice or Latin foods aisle in the supermarket) to this dish, but they're not necessary. If you do, reduce or omit the salt in step 4. Serve Puerto Rican Chicken Stew with cooked white rice and sliced avocado. **SERVES 4 TO 6**

ACTIVE TIME: 15 minutes **PRESSURE TIME:** 12 minutes
RELEASE METHOD: Manual **TOTAL TIME:** 45 minutes

---

1 (3- to 4-pound) chicken, cut into 8 pieces

Adobo powder (see Smart Tip) or salt

1 medium onion, chopped

5 cloves garlic, chopped

2 cubanelle peppers (or 1 green bell pepper), seeded and chopped

1 small tomato, seeded and chopped

6 tablespoons chopped cilantro, divided

3 tablespoons olive oil

1 teaspoon dried oregano

½ teaspoon ground cumin

¼ cup white wine (or more chicken broth)

1 large russet potato (about ¾ pound), peeled and cut into 1-inch cubes

2 carrots, peeled and sliced

¼ cup pimento-stuffed olives

1 (8-ounce) can tomato sauce

1 cup chicken broth

1 tablespoon chopped fresh oregano

Lime wedges, for serving (optional)

1. Season the chicken generously with adobo, and set it aside.

2. In a food processor, process the onion, garlic, cubanelle peppers, tomato, and 4 tablespoons of the cilantro until finely chopped.

3. Heat the oil in the inner pot on Sauté. Transfer the onion mixture to the pot, and cook, stirring constantly until much of the liquid has evaporated, about 3 minutes. Stir in the dried oregano and cumin. Add the wine, and cook until slightly reduced, about 3 minutes. Press Cancel.

4. Add the seasoned chicken, potato, carrots, olives, tomato sauce, broth and ½ teaspoon of salt. Stir to combine.

5. Lock the lid. Cook on high pressure for 12 minutes, then manually release the pressure.

6. Stir in the fresh oregano and remaining cilantro, and serve with lime wedges, if desired.

SMART TIP: Adobo powder is a delicious all-purpose seasoning salt made of garlic powder, oregano, and turmeric. It's available in most supermarkets in the Latin foods aisle. Once you try it, you may find yourself putting it on everything from baked chicken and broiled fish to roasted vegetables and stewed bean dishes. If you can't find it, just use salt and perhaps add a ¼ teaspoon garlic powder and an extra pinch of dried oregano to the liquid.

CHICKEN CACCIATORE

Chicken Cacciatore, or "hunter's style" chicken, is gently braised with tomatoes, wine, and herbs. Usually it takes about an hour on the stove, but with a multi-cooker you'll be ready to serve up an Italian feast in 30 minutes. Add a side of pasta and some crusty bread to sop up the sauce. **SERVES 4 TO 6**

ACTIVE TIME: 10 minutes **PRESSURE TIME:** 12 minutes
RELEASE METHOD: Manual **TOTAL TIME:** 30 minutes

---

1 whole chicken (about 3 pounds), cut into 8 pieces (you can also use an equal amount of chicken parts such as thighs)

Kosher salt and black pepper

2 tablespoons olive oil

1 onion, chopped

2 cloves garlic, minced

1 (14-ounce) can diced tomatoes

1 tablespoon tomato paste

½ cup white or red wine

½ cup chicken stock or water

½ teaspoon dried rosemary (crush the leaves between your fingers)

½ teaspoon dried oregano

2 tablespoons chopped fresh parsley, for garnish

1. Season the chicken generously with salt and pepper, and set it aside.

2. Heat the oil in the inner pot on Sauté. Add the onion and garlic and cook, stirring frequently until translucent, about 3 minutes. Press Cancel.

3. Add the seasoned chicken parts, tomatoes, tomato paste, wine, stock, rosemary, oregano, and 1 teaspoon of salt.

4. Lock the lid. Cook on high pressure for 12 minutes, then manually release the pressure. Stir in the chopped parsley.

CHICKEN WITH GARLIC

This dish is often called Chicken with Forty Cloves of Garlic, but there's nothing special about the number forty. You want about the equivalent of two to three heads of garlic, and the garlic just needs to be peeled, not chopped. (That's what keeps it nice and mellow in the sauce, instead of harsh and lingering.) Serve with crusty bread to spread the softened garlic on. If you wish, for a creamier version, you can stir in a few tablespoons of heavy cream after the chicken has finished cooking. **SERVES 4 TO 6**

ACTIVE TIME: 15 minutes **PRESSURE TIME:** 10 minutes
RELEASE METHOD: Manual **TOTAL TIME:** 35 minutes

---

8 bone-in chicken thighs (about 3 pounds)

Kosher salt and black pepper

1 tablespoon olive oil

40 cloves (approximately) garlic, peeled

1 rib celery, thinly sliced

3 sprigs fresh thyme, or 1 teaspoon dried thyme

1 pinch nutmeg (optional)

1 cup chicken broth

1 tablespoon cornstarch mixed with 1 tablespoon water

1. Season the chicken with salt and pepper, and set it aside.

2. Heat the oil in the inner pot on Sauté. Add the garlic and cook, stirring frequently until lightly golden brown. Press Cancel to stop the cooking. Do not overcook the garlic or it will taste bitter.

3. Add the chicken, celery, thyme, nutmeg (if using), broth, ½ teaspoon of salt, and ¼ teaspoon of pepper.

4. Lock the lid. Cook on high pressure for 10 minutes, then manually release the pressure.

5. Stir in the cornstarch mixture and cook until thickened, about 1 minute. If desired, remove the skin from the chicken.

SUPER-FAST TIP: Pick up peeled garlic at the supermarket to save yourself a lot of prep time.

CHICKEN AND RIESLING

Also known as *coq au Riesling*, Chicken and Riesling is a white-wine version of coq au vin. While a dry Riesling is traditional in this dish, you could certainly use another white wine; pinot grigio would be a good substitute. Serve this dish over buttered egg noodles or with potatoes. **SERVES 4 TO 6**

ACTIVE TIME: 15 minutes **PRESSURE TIME:** 10 minutes
RELEASE METHOD: Natural (10 minutes) **TOTAL TIME:** 55 minutes

---

6 bone-in, skinless chicken thighs (3 to 4 pounds)

Kosher salt and black pepper

1 teaspoon canola oil

2 slices bacon, chopped

1 clove garlic, chopped

1 large yellow onion, thinly sliced

2 large shallots, thinly sliced

1 (8-ounce) package cremini (baby bella) or white button mushrooms, sliced

1 cup dry Riesling

¼ cup heavy cream

2 tablespoons fresh chopped parsley

1. Season the chicken with salt and pepper, and set it aside.

2. Heat the oil in the inner pot on Sauté. Add the bacon and cook, stirring occasionally until browned, about 5 minutes. Add the garlic, onions, shallots, mushrooms, ½ teaspoon of salt, and ½ teaspoon of pepper, and cook, stirring occasionally, for 3 minutes. Stir in the wine and cook until fragrant, about 30 seconds. Press Cancel to stop the cooking process.

3. Nestle the chicken thighs into this mixture and spoon some of the liquid on top.

4. Lock the lid. Cook on high pressure for 10 minutes. Let the pressure release naturally for 10 minutes, then manually release any remaining pressure.

5. Reduce the sauce to the desired consistency. Stir in the heavy cream and parsley.

CHICKEN MARSALA

Chicken Marsala requires just a few ingredients but provides big flavor, thanks to the mushrooms and marsala wine. If there is a lot of liquid once you open the lid, remove the chicken and simmer the sauce for a few minutes to reduce it before stirring in the cornstarch slurry. **SERVES 4**

ACTIVE TIME: 15 minutes **PRESSURE TIME:** 8 minutes
RELEASE METHOD: Manual **TOTAL TIME:** 30 minutes

3 tablespoons unsalted butter, divided

8 ounces button or cremini (baby bella) mushrooms, sliced

2 cloves garlic, minced

Kosher salt and black pepper

½ cup marsala

4 boneless, skinless chicken breasts

½ cup chicken stock

2 tablespoons chopped parsley

1 tablespoon cornstarch mixed with 1 tablespoon water

1. Add the butter to the inner pot and heat on Sauté. Once the butter has melted and the foam has subsided, add the mushrooms and cook, stirring occasionally until browned and reduced, about 5 minutes. Stir in the garlic and the salt and pepper to taste.

2. Add the marsala to the pot and cook, using a wooden spoon to scrape up the brown bits at the bottom of the pot. Press Cancel to stop the cooking.

3. Season the chicken with salt and pepper. Add the chicken and stock to the pot.

4. Lock the lid. Cook on high pressure for 8 minutes, then manually release the pressure.

5. Transfer the chicken to a plate. Stir in the parsley and cornstarch mixture, and heat on Sauté until slightly thickened, about 1 to 2 minutes. Serve the sauce over the chicken.

TURKEY MEATLOAF

Meatloaf in the multi-cooker? Absolutely. The meatloaf cooks in a separate pan atop the steamer rack, and you just lift it out when it's done. Ground turkey helps keep it lighter than a beef meatloaf, and the cooking method ensures it turns out moist and delicious. **SERVES 4 TO 6**

ACTIVE TIME: 20 minutes **PRESSURE TIME:** 20 minutes
RELEASE METHOD: Manual **TOTAL TIME:** 50 minutes

2 tablespoons olive oil

½ onion, chopped

3 cloves garlic, minced

4 ounces white button or cremini (baby bella) mushrooms, chopped

Kosher salt and black pepper

1½ pounds ground turkey (preferably dark meat)

1 large egg, lightly beaten

2 teaspoons Worcestershire sauce

¼ cup bread crumbs

¼ cup grated Parmesan cheese

6 tablespoons ketchup, divided

2 tablespoons chopped fresh parsley

¼ teaspoon ground thyme

1. Grease a high-sided 7-inch round baking pan, and set it aside.

2. Heat the oil in the inner pot on Sauté. Add the onion, garlic, mushrooms, and ¼ teaspoon of the salt, and cook, stirring occasionally until the mushrooms are reduced, about 3 to 4 minutes. Transfer the ingredients to a plate to cool, and set aside. Wash and dry the pot.

3. Meanwhile, in a large bowl, gently mix together the ground turkey, egg, Worcestershire sauce, bread crumbs, Parmesan, 3 tablespoons of the ketchup, parsley, thyme, ½ teaspoon of salt, and ½ teaspoon of pepper. Mix in the now slightly cooled mushroom mixture until combined.

4. Transfer the mixture to the prepared pan and shape into a round loaf. Brush the loaf with the remaining 3 tablespoons ketchup.

5. Add 2 cups of water to the clean pot, and insert the steam rack.

6. Using a foil sling (see page 11), lower the pan into the inner pot, setting it down on the steam rack and tucking in the ends.

7. Lock the lid. Cook on high pressure for 20 minutes, then manually release the pressure. Check the meatloaf for doneness (165°F) using an instant-read thermometer. Carefully remove the meatloaf using the sling.

TURKEY "CROQUETTES"

Instead of being breaded and fried in oil, these leaner "croquettes" are simmered in their own sauce, which is then thickened to make a gravy. Serve this dish with mashed potatoes. **SERVES 4**

ACTIVE TIME: 15 minutes **PRESSURE TIME:** 5 minutes
RELEASE METHOD: Manual **TOTAL TIME:** 40 minutes

---

1 slice white bread, cubed

2–3 tablespoons milk

12 ounces ground turkey (preferably from dark meat)

½ onion, chopped

2 tablespoons finely chopped celery

1 large egg, lightly beaten

¾ teaspoon kosher salt

¼ teaspoon black pepper

2 tablespoons chopped fresh parsley, plus extra for garnish

2 teaspoons chopped fresh sage

1 cup chicken stock

1 tablespoon cornstarch mixed with 1 tablespoon water

1 tablespoon unsalted butter

1. Place the cubed bread in a small bowl with the milk. Stir to combine, and set aside while you mix the rest of the ingredients.

2. In a large bowl, loosely mix together the turkey, onion, celery, egg, salt, pepper, parsley, and sage. Mash the bread mixture with a fork and stir it into the meat mixture to combine.

3. Form the croquettes into 1½- to 2-inch long ovals.

4. Add the stock to the inner pot. Gently place the croquettes in a single layer on the bottom of the pot.

5. Lock the lid. Cook on high pressure for 5 minutes, then manually release the pressure.

6. Carefully transfer the croquettes to a serving dish.

7. Simmer the stock gently for a few minutes to reduce it to the desired consistency, then add the cornstarch mixture and stir until thickened. Press Cancel. Stir in the butter until melted. Serve the gravy over the croquettes and garnish with additional parsley.

SHREDDED TURKEY TACOS

These Shredded Turkey Tacos are perfect for when you get home from work and barely have enough energy to even think about dinner, let alone cook it. Just dump a few things together, measure a few spices, and close the pot. An easy, tasty dinner coming right up! **SERVES 4**

ACTIVE TIME: 5 minutes **PRESSURE TIME:** 15 minutes
RELEASE METHOD: Manual **TOTAL TIME:** 30 minutes

---

2 pounds bone-in turkey thighs, skin removed

1 (8-ounce) can tomato sauce

1 (7-ounce) can Mexican salsa verde

¼ cup water

1 small onion, chopped

1 tablespoon Worcestershire sauce or soy sauce

2 tablespoons chili powder

½ teaspoon ground oregano

½ teaspoon garlic powder

¼ teaspoon kosher salt

Soft corn or flour tortillas, for serving

Shredded cheddar or Monterey Jack, for serving

Shredded lettuce, for serving

Sour cream, for serving

1. Add all of the ingredients to the multi-cooker, and stir to combine.

2. Lock the lid. Cook on high pressure for 15 minutes, then manually release the pressure. Check the turkey for doneness.

3. Using two forks, shred the turkey. Serve on tortillas with shredded cheese, lettuce, and sour cream.

BEEF, PORK, AND LAMB

WEEKNIGHT POT ROAST

There's not much that's speedy about most pot roast recipes. Depending on the size of the roast, it can take anywhere from two to four hours to cook. But by cutting the roast into large chunks and cooking it under pressure, you can have a classic comfort dish on the table in about a half an hour. Serve this dish with boiled or roasted potatoes. **SERVES 6**

ACTIVE TIME: 10 minutes **PRESSURE TIME:** 20 minutes
RELEASE METHOD: Manual **TOTAL TIME:** 30 minutes

---

1 (3-pound) boneless beef chuck roast, cut into 1½-inch chunks

Kosher salt and black pepper

2 onions, chopped

2 large carrots, peeled and sliced into ½-inch-thick rounds

2 ribs celery, chopped

4 cloves garlic, crushed

½ teaspoon dried thyme

2 tablespoons tomato paste

1 tablespoon soy sauce or Worcestershire sauce

½ cup chicken broth

½ cup dry red wine

2 tablespoons chopped fresh parsley

Boiled or roasted potatoes, for serving

1. Season the beef with salt and pepper, and set it aside.

2. Add the onions, carrots, celery, garlic, thyme, tomato paste, soy sauce, broth, wine, 1 teaspoon of salt, and ½ teaspoon of pepper to the inner pot, and stir to combine.

3. Lock the lid. Cook on high pressure for 20 minutes, then manually release the pressure. The beef should break apart easily when pierced with a fork. If not, return to high pressure for another 5 minutes.

4. Stir in the parsley and serve with a side of potatoes.

SIRLOIN TIPS IN MUSHROOM AND ONION GRAVY

The secret to this recipe is the dried onion bits, which amp up the onion flavor without a gravy seasoning packet full of mystery ingredients you can't pronounce. Serve this dish over mashed potatoes with gravy. A side of steamed peas is a classic and delicious addition. **SERVES 4**

ACTIVE TIME: 10 minutes **PRESSURE TIME:** 10 minutes
RELEASE METHOD: Manual **TOTAL TIME:** 30 minutes

1½ pounds beef tips

Kosher salt and black pepper

2 onions, thinly sliced

8 ounces white or cremini (baby bella) mushrooms, thinly sliced

2 tablespoons dried minced onion

1½ teaspoons finely chopped thyme leaves

¼ cup dry sherry

1 cup beef broth

1 tablespoon cornstarch mixed with 2 tablespoons water

1. Season the beef with salt and pepper. Add the beef to the pot along with the onions, mushrooms, dried onion, thyme, ½ teaspoon of salt, ½ teaspoon of pepper, sherry, and beef broth.

2. Lock the lid. Cook on high pressure for 10 minutes, then manually release the pressure.

3. Using a slotted spoon, remove the beef to a bowl and tent the meat with aluminum foil. Simmer the sauce until it reaches the desired consistency. Stir in the cornstarch mixture and cook until thickened, about 1 minute. Return the beef to the pot to coat with the gravy before serving.

THAI RED CURRY BEEF

Thai red curry paste pairs nicely with beef, and the combination of sweet potatoes, coconut milk, and fresh basil makes a satisfyingly complex medley of flavors you'll crave again and again. **SERVES 4 TO 6**

ACTIVE TIME: 10 minutes **PRESSURE TIME:** 15 minutes
RELEASE: Natural (5 minutes) **TOTAL TIME:** 40 minutes

1½ pounds boneless beef short ribs, cut into 1-inch chunks

1 sweet potato, peeled and cut into 1-inch chunks

1 red bell pepper, seeded and sliced

1 onion, thinly sliced

2 tablespoons red curry paste (or more to taste)

¾ cup coconut milk

¼ cup beef or chicken stock

2 tablespoons fish sauce

2 tablespoons packed brown sugar

½ cup lightly packed basil (preferably Thai basil), thinly sliced, divided

Cooked jasmine rice, for serving

1. Add the beef, sweet potato, pepper, onion, curry paste, coconut milk, stock, fish sauce, and brown sugar to the inner pot. Stir to combine.

2. Lock the lid. Cook on high pressure for 15 minutes. Let the pressure release naturally for 5 minutes, then manually release any remaining pressure.

3. Stir in the basil. If using Thai basil, which is sturdier than regular basil, simmer for a few minutes to release the licorice flavor.

4. Serve the curry over jasmine rice.

CLASSIC BEEF STEW

It may not be flashy, but it's comforting and delicious and a perfect match for the multi-cooker, so why not revisit beef stew? Serve Classic Beef Stew with a robust red wine, such as red zinfandel or cabernet sauvignon, a big green salad, and lots of mashed potatoes or buttered noodles. Sop up the gravy with a crusty bread. **SERVES 4 TO 6**

ACTIVE TIME: 10 minutes **PRESSURE TIME:** 15 minutes
RELEASE METHOD: Natural (10 minutes) **TOTAL TIME:** 45 minutes

---

2 pounds beef stew meat, cut into 1-inch cubes

Kosher salt and black pepper

1 tablespoon olive oil, plus more as needed

½ cup dry red wine

1 pound potatoes, peeled and cut into 1-inch cubes

2 carrots, peeled and sliced

1 large onion, chopped

1 rib celery, sliced into ¼-inch-thick slices

2½ cups beef or chicken stock

2 tablespoons tomato paste

2 teaspoons fresh chopped thyme leaves

1. Season the beef with salt and pepper. Heat the oil in the inner pot on Sauté. Working in batches if necessary to avoid crowding the pan, brown the beef on all sides. If working in batches, transfer the browned meat to a plate while you brown the rest. Add more oil to the pan if necessary to keep the meat from sticking.

2. Add the wine and cook, using a wooden spoon to loosen the brown bits at the bottom of the pan until slightly reduced, about 3 minutes. Press Cancel to stop the cooking process.

3. Add all the beef and the remaining ingredients to the pot along with 1 teaspoon of salt and ½ teaspoon of pepper. Stir to combine.

4. Lock the lid. Cook on high pressure for 15 minutes. Let the pressure release naturally for 10 minutes, then manually release any remaining pressure.

5. If needed, simmer the sauce on Sauté for a few minutes, stirring regularly until slightly thickened.

SMART TIP: Stir in 1 cup of thawed frozen peas at the end.

SHREDDED CHIPOTLE BEEF

Shredded Chipotle Beef is spicy and smoky with a cooked-all-day taste that's hard to believe you achieved in such a short time! Serve with soft flour or corn tortillas, fresh pico de gallo, sliced avocado, and sour cream. **SERVES 4 TO 6**

ACTIVE TIME: 10 minutes **PRESSURE TIME:** 15 minutes
METHOD: Natural (10 minutes) **TOTAL TIME:** 45 minutes

1 (approximately 1¾-pound) flank steak, cut into ½-inch-wide x 2-inch-long strips

Kosher salt and black pepper

2 tablespoons olive oil

4 cloves garlic, minced

1 chipotle pepper in adobo sauce, minced (from a can)

1 teaspoon paprika

½ teaspoon dried oregano

2 red bell peppers, seeded and thinly sliced

1 large onion, halved and thinly sliced

½ cup tomato sauce

½ cup beef or chicken stock or water

1. Season the steak with salt and pepper. Heat the oil in the inner pot on Sauté. Working in batches to avoid crowding the pan, brown the beef on all sides. Add all the steak and the remaining ingredients and ½ teaspoon of salt to the pot. Stir to combine.

2. Lock the lid. Cook on high pressure for 15 minutes. Let the pressure release naturally for 10 minutes, then manually release any remaining pressure.

3. Simmer on Sauté, stirring regularly until the sauce is thickened to the desired consistency, about 5 minutes. Using two forks, shred the beef.

SUPER FAST
INSTANT POT
PRESSURE
COOKER
COOKBOOK

100

SMOTHERED PORK CHOPS IN ONION GRAVY

There's something so satisfying about tender pork chops simmered in savory onion gravy. Make lots of fluffy mashed potatoes so that you can enjoy more of the gravy goodness. **SERVES 4**

ACTIVE TIME: 20 minutes **PRESSURE TIME:** 8 minutes
RELEASE METHOD: Natural (5 minutes) **TOTAL TIME:** 50 minutes

4 large bone-in pork chops (about 2½ pounds)

Kosher salt and black pepper

2 tablespoons olive oil

2 large onions, thinly sliced

¼ cup dry white wine

4 cloves garlic, peeled and smashed

2 tablespoons dried minced onion

½ teaspoon ground thyme

1 cup chicken stock

1 tablespoon cornstarch mixed with 2 tablespoons water

1. Season the pork chops generously with salt and pepper, and set them aside.

2. Heat the oil in the inner pot on Sauté. Add the onions and cook, stirring frequently until golden brown, about 10 minutes. Add the wine and garlic, and stir with a wooden spoon to loosen up the brown bits. Stir in the dried onion and thyme. Add the seasoned pork chops and stock, and stir the ingredients to combine.

3. Lock the lid. Cook on high pressure for 8 minutes. Let the pressure release naturally for 5 minutes, then manually release any remaining pressure.

4. Transfer the pork chops to a plate. Press Sauté, and let the sauce simmer for a few minutes, stirring occasionally until slightly reduced. Stir in the cornstarch mixture and cook until thickened. Serve the pork chops over mashed potatoes with a generous ladle of onion gravy.

PORK TENDERLOIN WITH CREAMY GARLIC FENNEL SAUCE

Fennel has a mild licorice flavor that mellows even further in this simple but delicate sauce. The fennel can be served crunchy and raw, but it gets wonderfully tender when cooked under pressure along with the pork. **SERVES 4**

ACTIVE TIME: 15 minutes **PRESSURE TIME:** 5 minutes
RELEASE METHOD: Natural (10 minutes) **TOTAL TIME:** 40 minutes

1 pork tenderloin (about 1½ pounds), cut into 4 equal pieces

Kosher salt and black pepper

1 tablespoon olive oil

4 cloves garlic, thinly sliced

½ cup chicken stock

½ cup white wine

1 bulb fennel, halved and thinly sliced, feathery green leaves reserved for garnish

¼ cup heavy cream

1. Season the pork with salt and pepper. Heat the oil in the pot on Sauté. Add the pork and brown on all sides, about 5 minutes. Remove the pork, and set it aside. Add the garlic and stir until fragrant, about 30 seconds.

2. Stir in the stock and wine, and use a wooden spoon to scrape up any brown bits on the bottom of the pot. Press Cancel to stop the cooking.

3. Return the pork and any accumulated juiced to the pot, along with the fennel. Stir the ingredients to combine.

4. Lock the lid. Cook on low pressure for 5 minutes. Let the pressure release naturally for 10 minutes, then manually release any remaining pressure.

5. Transfer the pork to a plate, and tent the meat loosely with foil. Sauté the pan juices until reduced by nearly half, about 5 minutes. Stir in the heavy cream. Season to taste with salt and pepper.

6. Slice the now-rested pork, and spoon the fennel sauce over the top to serve.

SUPER FAST
INSTANT POT
PRESSURE
COOKER
COOKBOOK

102

GARLICKY SAGE PORK TENDERLOIN

Pork tenderloin is a lean cut that cooks quickly in the multi-cooker. Pork has a natural flavor affinity with apples, so the sauce here is made with hard apple cider. You could also use white wine. **SERVES 4 TO 6**

> **ACTIVE TIME:** 15 minutes **PRESSURE TIME:** 5 minutes
> **RELEASE METHOD:** Natural (10 minutes) **TOTAL TIME:** 40 minutes

3 cloves garlic, minced

2 teaspoons chopped fresh sage, minced

2 tablespoons olive oil, divided

Kosher salt and black pepper

1 pork tenderloin (about 1½ pounds), cut into 4 equal pieces

½ cup hard apple cider

½ cup chicken stock

1 sprig thyme

2 tablespoons unsalted butter

Lemon wedges, for serving

1. Mix together the garlic, sage, 1 tablespoon of the oil, ½ teaspoon salt, and ½ teaspoon pepper in a small bowl to form a paste.

2. Using a knife tip, cut small slits (about ½-inch deep) into the loin pieces, and insert a little bit of the paste into each opening. Rub any remaining paste all over the outside of the meat.

3. Heat the remaining tablespoon of oil in the inner pot on Sauté. Add the loin pieces and cook, turning occasionally, until golden brown in spots. Transfer the pork to a plate, and set aside.

4. Stir in the cider, stock, and thyme sprig and use a wooden spoon to scrape up the brown bits. Press Cancel to stop the cooking.

5. Return the pork, along with any accumulated juices, to the pot.

6. Lock the lid. Cook on low pressure for 5 minutes. Let the pressure release naturally for 10 minutes, then manually release any remaining pressure.

7. Remove the pork to a plate, tent the meat with foil, and set the pot to Sauté. Reduce the sauce, stirring frequently, about 5 minutes. Stir in the butter, and add salt and pepper to taste. Serve the sauce over the pork with a side of lemon wedges.

ROPA VIEJA

If you haven't had Ropa Vieja before, it's essentially like beef stew, but Cuban style. *Ropa vieja* literally means "old clothes" in Spanish, and it's a colorfully fun name for this delicious shredded beef dish. Traditionally, ropa vieja uses flank steak, which braises for several hours until it falls apart. This weeknight version is just as satisfying, but uses tasty boneless short ribs, which are cut into big chunks to cook much faster. Serve with rice or potatoes and cubed avocado. **SERVES 4**

ACTIVE TIME: 15 minutes **PRESSURE TIME:** 15 minutes
RELEASE: Natural (10 minutes) **TOTAL TIME:** 45 minutes

---

1 tablespoon olive oil

1 large onion, halved and thinly sliced

1 cubanelle or red bell pepper, seeded and sliced

2 carrots, peeled and thinly sliced

1 rib celery, finely chopped

5 cloves garlic, thinly sliced

½ teaspoon cumin

¼ teaspoon dried oregano

2 pounds boneless beef short ribs, cut into 1-inch chunks

Adobo powder (see Smart Tip page 81) or kosher salt

Black pepper

2 to 3 tablespoons green pimento-stuffed olives

1 (8-ounce) can tomato sauce

½ cup beef or chicken stock

1 bay leaf (optional)

¼ cup chopped fresh cilantro or parsley, divided

1. Heat the oil in the inner pot on Sauté. Add the onion, cubanelle pepper, carrots, and celery, and cook, stirring occasionally, about 2 to 3 minutes. Stir in the garlic and cook until fragrant, 30 seconds. Press Cancel to stop the cooking. Add the cumin and oregano, and stir to coat.

2. Season the short ribs with adobo and black pepper, and add them to the pot along with the olives, tomato sauce, stock, bay leaf (if using), and ½ teaspoon of salt.

3. Lock the lid. Cook on high pressure for 15 minutes. Allow the pressure to release naturally for 10 minutes, then manually release any remaining pressure. Stir in the cilantro before serving.

WEEKNIGHT PULLED PORK

Pulled pork, a favorite for summer picnics, is generally not a candidate for weeknight dinners because it takes hours and hours to cook. This super-quick version allows you to revisit summer any time of the week—or year. Plan a picnic night, either indoors or out, and serve this pork with other al fresco favorites, such as coleslaw and macaroni salad. You can also prepare a side, such as Picnic Bean Salad (page 125) the day before. Serve the pork on a Kaiser roll with a slather of mustard and a few slices of pickles or pickled jalapeño. **SERVES 4 TO 6**

ACTIVE TIME: 10 minutes **PRESSURE TIME:** 15 minutes
RELEASE METHOD: Manual **TOTAL TIME:** 35 minutes

---

1 tablespoon packed brown sugar

2 teaspoons paprika

2 teaspoons chili powder

1 teaspoon ground cumin

½ teaspoon onion powder

¼ teaspoon dried oregano

1 teaspoon kosher salt

1 teaspoon coarsely ground black pepper

1 pinch (or to taste) cayenne pepper

2 pounds (trimmed weight) boneless pork shoulder or butt, trimmed of fat and cut into 2-inch chunks

¾ cup barbecue sauce (homemade or your favorite store-bought brand)

1 tablespoon apple cider vinegar

1 cup beer, such as a lager

1. In a small bowl, mix together the spices. In a large bowl, toss the pork with the spice mix, rubbing to coat. Stir in the barbecue sauce and vinegar.

2. Add the beer to the inner pot and stir in the pork.

3. Lock the lid. Cook on high pressure for 15 minutes, then manually release the pressure. The pork should fall apart when pierced with a fork. If not, cook under high pressure for another 5 minutes.

4. Using two forks, shred the pork. Stir to coat in the sauce, and serve. If needed, simmer the sauce for a few minutes to help it thicken.

SUPER FAST
INSTANT POT
PRESSURE
COOKER
COOKBOOK

106

ITALIAN SAUSAGE AND LENTILS

Just as with the Chorizo and Chickpea Stew (page 108), the sausage here provides major flavor to the beans (or, in this case, lentils), making this simple dish perfect for when you don't have a lot of time or energy but still need to get a tasty, wholesome dinner on the table. **SERVES 4**

ACTIVE TIME: 10 minutes **PRESSURE TIME:** 10 minutes
RELEASE METHOD: Natural (10 minutes) **TOTAL TIME:** 40 minutes

2 tablespoons olive oil

4 links mild or hot Italian sausage, pricked with a fork

1 onion, chopped

4 cloves garlic, thinly sliced

¾ cup dry red wine

1 cup green or brown lentils, picked over for stones and rinsed

1 cup chicken stock

2 teaspoons chopped fresh thyme

2 tablespoons chopped fresh basil or parsley

Kosher salt and black pepper

1. Heat the oil in the inner pot on Sauté. Sear the sausages until brown, about 3 minutes per side. Transfer them to a plate, and set it aside.

2. Add the onion and garlic and cook, stirring frequently until the onion is translucent, about 3 minutes. Stir in the wine, and using a wooden spoon, loosen the brown bits from the pan. Press Cancel to stop the cooking process.

3. Return the sausages and any accumulated juices to the pan. Add the lentils, stock, and thyme. Stir to combine.

4. Lock the lid. Cook on high pressure for 10 minutes. Let the pressure release naturally for 10 minutes, then manually release any remaining pressure.

5. Stir in the basil, and season to taste if needed with salt and pepper.

CHORIZO AND CHICKPEA STEW

There's just something so satisfying about the pairing of chorizo and chickpeas. Plus, because the chorizo is so highly seasoned, it does most of the heavy lifting flavor-wise so that you don't need to add much else in the way of spices. Make sure to use fresh chorizo sausage from the refrigerated case, not the cured ready-to-eat kind. **SERVES 4**

ACTIVE TIME: 15 minutes **PRESSURE TIME:** 5 minutes
RELEASE: Natural (10 minutes) **TOTAL TIME:** 40 minutes

---

1 (29-ounce) can chickpeas, drained and rinsed

3 fresh chorizo sausages, cut into 1-inch slices

1 large onion, chopped

2 cubanelle peppers (or 1 red bell pepper), seeded and thinly sliced

5 cloves garlic, thinly sliced

1 (8-ounce) can tomato sauce

1 cup chicken stock

2 tablespoons tomato paste

½ teaspoon dried oregano

¼ cup chopped fresh cilantro, divided

Kosher salt, if needed

1. Add the chickpeas, sausage, onion, cubanelle peppers, garlic, tomato sauce, stock, tomato paste, oregano, and 2 tablespoons of the cilantro to the multi-cooker. Stir to combine.

2. Lock the lid. Cook on high pressure for 5 minutes. Allow the pressure to release naturally for 10 minutes, then release any remaining pressure.

3. Stir in the remaining cilantro. Taste and add salt if needed. The sausage and broth are usually salty enough that additional seasoning is not required.

SUPER FAST
INSTANT POT
PRESSURE
COOKER
COOKBOOK

108

SAUCY MEMPHIS-STYLE RIBS

If you're hungry for ribs and don't want to waste several hours making them in the oven, give these much quicker Saucy Memphis-Style Ribs a try. Feel free to substitute your favorite homemade barbecue sauce recipe for the prepared version called for below. Don't forget the extra napkins—you'll need them! **SERVES 4**

ACTIVE TIME: 20 minutes **PRESSURE TIME:** 30 minutes
RELEASE: Manual **TOTAL TIME:** 60 minutes

---

1 tablespoon brown sugar

2 teaspoons paprika

1 teaspoon garlic powder

½ teaspoon dried oregano

½ teaspoon salt

½ teaspoon coarsely ground black pepper

1 cup barbecue sauce, divided

¼ cup tomato sauce

3 pounds St. Louis–style pork ribs, cut into 2-inch rib segments

1 cup water

1. In a small bowl, mix together the spices. In another small bowl, mix together ½ cup of the barbecue sauce with the tomato sauce.

2. Remove the membrane from the ribs and discard. Rub the spice mixture into the ribs, then toss the ribs with the barbecue sauce mixture.

3. Add the water and the ribs to the pot.

4. Lock the lid. Cook on high pressure for 30 minutes, then manually release the pressure. The ribs should be fork-tender.

5. Meanwhile, preheat the broiler. Transfer the ribs to a baking sheet and brush the tops with some of the remaining barbecue sauce. Broil until caramelized, about 3 to 5 minutes. Flip and repeat on the other side.

SUPER-FAST TIP: Separating the ribs helps them to cook faster.

BEEF BURGUNDY

Beef Burgundy, or boeuf bourguignon, is a traditional French beef and red wine dish. Typically, as the name suggests, the beef is braised in Burgundy wine, but you can certainly use a different red wine that you have on hand. Just make sure it's one you wouldn't mind drinking as well—that is, don't use a cooking wine. **SERVES 4 TO 6**

ACTIVE TIME: 15 minutes **PRESSURE TIME:** 15 minutes
RELEASE METHOD: Natural (10 minutes) **TOTAL TIME:** 40 minutes

2 pounds boneless beef short ribs, cut into 1-inch chunks

Kosher salt and black pepper

¼ cup all-purpose flour

1 teaspoon olive oil

2 slices bacon, chopped

1 cup dry red wine

1 cup beef broth

1 tablespoon tomato paste

1½ cups frozen pearl onions

8 ounces white button mushrooms, sliced

2 carrots, peeled and thinly sliced

1 bay leaf

½ teaspoon dried thyme

2 tablespoons minced fresh parsley for garnish

1. Season the beef chunks with salt and pepper. Dredge the meat in the flour, and set it aside.

2. Heat the oil in the inner pot on Sauté. Add the bacon and cook, stirring occasionally until browned, 3 to 4 minutes. Using a slotted spoon, transfer the bacon to a paper towel–lined plate to drain.

3. Working in batches if necessary, add the beef and brown on all sides, 4 to 5 minutes.

4. Stir in the red wine and broth. Using a wooden spoon, loosen the brown bits at the bottom of the pot.

5. Stir in any reserved beef along with the tomato paste, onions, mushrooms, carrots, bay leaf, thyme, ½ teaspoon of salt, and ¼ teaspoon of pepper.

6. Lock the lid. Cook on high pressure for 15 minutes. Let the pressure release naturally for 10 minutes, then manually release any remaining pressure. If the liquid is too thin, cook it on Sauté for a few minutes until it reaches the desired consistency. Stir in the parsley, and season to taste with salt and pepper. Sprinkle the dish with the reserved bacon bits.

SUPER FAST
INSTANT POT
PRESSURE
COOKER
COOKBOOK

110

GREEN CHILE PORK

Jarred salsa verde, a tomatillo-based salsa, is your shortcut to super-simple and super-fast Green Chile Pork. A touch of honey softens the tang of the salsa and tomatoes. Just shred the pork when it's finished, and serve it with tortillas or rice. **SERVES 4**

> **ACTIVE TIME:** 10 minutes **PRESSURE TIME:** 15 minutes
> **RELEASE METHOD:** Natural (10 minutes) **TOTAL TIME:** 45 minutes

2 pounds boneless pork shoulder, cut into 1-inch chunks

Kosher salt and black pepper

1 (16-ounce) jar salsa verde

1 (14.5) ounce can diced tomatoes, drained

1 tablespoon honey

1 teaspoon ground cumin

1 teaspoon dried oregano

½ cup chicken stock

¼ cup chopped fresh cilantro leaves

1. Season the pork with salt and pepper. Add it to the pot, along with the salsa verde, tomatoes, honey, cumin, oregano, and stock.

2. Lock the lid. Cook on high pressure for 15 minutes. Let the pressure release naturally for 10 minutes, then manually release any remaining pressure.

3. If needed, reduce the sauce to the desired consistency. Shred the pork using two forks, and stir in the cilantro.

SUPER FAST
INSTANT POT
PRESSURE
COOKER
COOKBOOK

112

MOO SHU PORK

Moo Shu Pork is a Chinese restaurant favorite featuring tender pork, crunchy cabbage, and salty-sweet hoisin sauce. Make it at home in just a few minutes with the pressure cooker. Dried shiitake mushrooms add a delicious umami boost, and you don't even have to soak them first! **SERVES 4**

ACTIVE TIME: 15 minutes **PRESSURE TIME:** 8 minutes
RELEASE METHOD: Manual **TOTAL TIME:** 35 minutes

1½ pounds boneless pork shoulder, cut into thin strips, about ¼-inch wide by 2-inches long

½ ounce dried shiitake mushrooms, stems removed and tops broken into pieces

½ cup chicken stock

¼ cup soy sauce

¼ cup dry sherry or more chicken stock

1 tablespoon sesame oil

3 cloves garlic, minced

3 cups sliced cabbage or coleslaw mix

1 tablespoon cornstarch mixed with 1 tablespoon water

Flour tortillas, for serving

Hoisin sauce, for serving

1 cup thinly sliced scallions, for serving

1. Add the pork to the inner pot, along with the mushrooms, stock, soy sauce, sherry, sesame oil, and garlic. Stir to combine.

2. Lock the lid. Cook on high pressure for 8 minutes, then manually release the pressure.

3. Stir in the cabbage. Cook for a few minutes on Sauté, stirring frequently until slightly softened but still crunchy. Stir in the cornstarch mixture, and cook until thickened, 1 to 2 minutes.

4. Serve on tortillas with hoisin sauce and sliced scallions.

OREGANO GARLIC LAMB

Oregano Garlic Lamb is spiked with Greek-inspired flavors. The lemon and white wine help to cut some of the richness of the lamb, and the minced garlic added at the end boosts the garlicky punch of the sauce. Serve this dish with roasted potatoes. **SERVES 4**

ACTIVE TIME: 15 minutes PRESSURE TIME: 15 minutes
RELEASE METHOD: Manual TOTAL TIME: 40 minutes

2 pounds boneless leg of lamb, cut into 1-inch chunks

Kosher salt and black pepper

2 tablespoons olive oil, plus more as needed

6 cloves garlic (5 cloves thinly sliced and 1 clove minced), divided

1½ teaspoons dried oregano

2 tablespoons lemon juice

½ cup chicken stock

½ cup white wine

Lemon wedges, for serving

1. Generously season the lamb chunks with salt and pepper. Heat the oil in the inner pot on Sauté. Working in batches to avoid crowding the pan, sear the lamb chunks until well browned and golden on all sides. Transfer the meat to a plate to rest while you finish the remaining lamb.

2. Press Cancel. Add 5 cloves of the garlic to the pot, and cook using the residual heat until fragrant, about 30 seconds. Return the lamb and any accumulated juices to the pot along with the oregano, lemon juice, stock, and wine.

3. Lock the lid. Cook on high pressure for 15 minutes, then manually release the pressure.

4. The lamb should be tender when pierced with a fork. If not, return to high pressure for 5 additional minutes. Reduce the liquid on simmer until it's the consistency of a glaze. Season the dish to taste, and stir in the remaining minced garlic. Serve, preferably with some oven-roasted potatoes and a side of lemon wedges.

SUPER FAST
INSTANT POT
PRESSURE
COOKER
COOKBOOK

114

RED WINE-BRAISED LEG OF LAMB

Leg of lamb in under an hour? It's absolutely possible with the multi-cooker when you use boneless leg of lamb cut into chunks. Serve this hearty, elegant classic with buttered noodles, polenta, or mashed potatoes. **SERVES 4**

ACTIVE TIME: 10 minutes **PRESSURE TIME:** 15 minutes
RELEASE METHOD: Natural (10 minutes) **TOTAL TIME:** 45 minutes

---

2 pounds boneless leg of lamb, cut into 1-inch chunks

Kosher salt and black pepper

1 tablespoon olive oil

5 cloves garlic, thinly sliced

1 cup red wine

1 cup peeled pearl onions, or 2 small shallots, chopped

2 carrots, peeled and chopped

1 teaspoon finely chopped fresh rosemary

2 teaspoons finely chopped fresh thyme

1 teaspoon finely chopped fresh oregano

½ cup chicken stock

2 tablespoons tomato paste

1. Season the lamb with salt and pepper. Heat the olive oil in the inner pot on Sauté. Working in batches to avoid crowding the pan, brown the lamb chunks on all sides. Transfer the meat to a plate, and set it aside.

2. Stir in the garlic and cook until fragrant, 30 seconds. Stir in the wine, and using a wooden spoon, scrape up the brown bits on the bottom of the pot. Press Cancel to stop the cooking.

3. Add the lamb and any accumulated juices back to the pot along with the remaining ingredients and 1 teaspoon of salt. Stir to combine.

4. Lock the lid. Cook on high pressure for 15 minutes. Let the pressure release naturally for 10 minutes, then manually release any remaining pressure.

5. Test the lamb for doneness. It should be fork-tender. If it is still firm, return to high pressure for several minutes.

SIMPLE
SIDES

FOURTH OF JULY POTATO SALAD

The genius of this recipe is that you cook the potatoes *and* hard-boil the eggs together in the multi-cooker—in just 5 minutes—saving you time, dishes, and extra steps. You'll discover that the potatoes, which never touch the water, come out extra smooth and creamy! Give this Fourth of July Potato Salad a try, and you may never make potato salad any other way again. **SERVES 4**

ACTIVE TIME: 15 minutes   **PRESSURE TIME:** 5 minutes
RELEASE METHOD: Manual   **TOTAL TIME:** 30 minutes (plus refrigerating time)

1½ pounds Yukon gold or red bliss potatoes, peeled and cut into large chunks

2 large eggs

½ small red onion, minced

1 rib celery, minced

2 tablespoons finely chopped parsley

1–2 tablespoons sweet pickle relish (optional)

Kosher salt and black pepper

1½ tablespoons white wine vinegar

½ cup mayonnaise

3 scallions, sliced

1. Insert the steam rack into the inner pot and add 2 cups of water. Place a stainless-steel steamer basket (see page 11) on top of the rack and carefully add the potato chunks and eggs.

2. Lock the lid. Cook on high pressure for 5 minutes, then manually release the pressure.

3. Meanwhile, stir together the onion, celery, parsley, sweet pickle relish (if using), ¼ teaspoon of salt, and ½ teaspoon of pepper in a large bowl.

4. Using a large slotted spoon, carefully transfer the eggs to a bowl of ice water to cool.

5. Transfer the potatoes to a separate bowl and sprinkle evenly with the vinegar. Gently mix the potatoes with the other ingredients. Set the mixture aside to cool slightly and marinate.

6. When the eggs are cool enough to handle, peel and chop them. Add the chopped eggs to the potato mixture along with the mayonnaise and scallions, and fold to combine. Season the dish to taste with more salt and pepper, if needed.

7. Keep the potato salad refrigerated until ready to serve.

SUPER FAST
INSTANT POT
PRESSURE
COOKER
COOKBOOK

118

FRENCH POTATO SALAD

With no mayo, lots of herbs, and a vinaigrette dressing, French Potato Salad bears little resemblance to its American cousin. It's tangy and creamy and incredibly versatile—you can serve it warm or cold, and it tastes even better the next day after the herbs have had a chance to hang out with and flavor the potatoes! **SERVES 6**

ACTIVE TIME: 10 minutes **PRESSURE TIME:** 5 minutes
RELEASE METHOD: Manual **TOTAL TIME:** 25 minutes

1½ pounds fingerling potatoes, halved

3 large eggs

3 tablespoons olive oil

1 clove garlic, finely minced

1 small shallot, minced

1 tablespoon grainy or smooth Dijon mustard

¼ cup mixed chopped fresh herbs, such as chives, dill, basil, and/or parsley

Kosher salt and black pepper

2 teaspoons white wine vinegar, plus more as needed

1. Insert the steam rack into the multi-cooker and add 2 cups of water. Place a stainless-steel steamer basket (see page 11) on top of the rack and carefully add the potatoes and eggs.

2. Lock the lid. Cook on high pressure for 5 minutes, then manually release the pressure.

3. Transfer the eggs to a bowl of ice water to cool.

4. Meanwhile, in a small bowl, stir together the oil, garlic, shallot, mustard, herbs, ¼ teaspoon of salt, and ¼ teaspoon of pepper.

5. Transfer the warm potatoes to a large bowl, and toss immediately with the vinegar. Add the remaining dressing, and stir to coat. Taste and add more vinegar or salt if needed. Serve warm or cold.

SUPER FAST
INSTANT POT
PRESSURE
COOKER
COOKBOOK

120

BUTTERMILK MASHED POTATOES

Buttermilk just seems to make everything taste better. Think biscuits, pancakes, fried chicken. . . and these creamy Buttermilk Mashed Potatoes! **SERVES 4**

ACTIVE TIME: 10 minutes   **PRESSURE TIME:** 5 minutes
RELEASE METHOD: Manual   **TOTAL TIME:** 25 minutes

---

2 pounds floury potatoes, such as russet or Idaho, peeled and cut into 1-inch cubes

¼ cup (4 tablespoons) unsalted butter, melted

¾–1 cup buttermilk

Kosher salt and black pepper

Chives, for garnish

1. Insert the steam rack into the multi-cooker and add 2 cups of water. Place a stainless-steel steamer basket (see page 11) on top of the rack and add the potatoes.

2. Lock the lid. Cook on high pressure for 5 minutes, then manually release the pressure.

3. Transfer the potatoes to a large bowl and mash with a potato masher or press through a potato ricer. Stir in the butter and ¾ cup of buttermilk, adding more if necessary to achieve the desired consistency. Season with salt and pepper to taste, and garnish with chives. Serve immediately.

ROSEMARY POLENTA

This rosemary-spiked polenta is great with grilled Italian sausages and a nice marinara sauce. It makes a nice alternative to the pasta routine and is almost as simple to whip up. **SERVES 4**

ACTIVE TIME: 5 minutes **PRESSURE TIME:** 10 minutes
RELEASE METHOD: Natural (15 minutes) **TOTAL TIME:** 40 minutes

---

4 tablespoons unsalted butter, divided

2 tablespoons minced onion

3 cloves garlic, minced

2 teaspoons chopped fresh rosemary (or ½ teaspoon dried)

1 cup polenta (not quick cooking or instant)

Kosher salt

4½ cups water

½ cup grated Parmesan cheese

1. Add 2 tablespoons of the butter to the inner pot and heat on Sauté. Once the butter has melted, add the onion and garlic and cook, stirring frequently, about 2 to 3 minutes. Press Cancel to stop the cooking. Stir in the rosemary.

2. Add the polenta, 1 teaspoon of salt, and the water, and stir to combine.

3. Lock the lid. Cook on high pressure for 10 minutes. Let the pressure release naturally for 15 minutes, then manually release any remaining pressure. (See Smart Tip.) Stir well.

4. Stir in the Parmesan and remaining butter, and serve immediately.

SMART TIP: You can try releasing the pressure sooner than 15 minutes, but do so slowly and be prepared to stop and wait if the valve starts to spit.

EASY CABBAGE "STIR FRY"

This (mostly) hands-off Asian-inspired "stir-fry" would be a great side dish for a night you're making a main course that requires more of your attention. It's also a good use for that big head of cabbage you got on super sale at the grocery store. **SERVES 4 TO 6**

ACTIVE TIME: 15 minutes **PRESSURE TIME:** 3 minutes
RELEASE METHOD: Manual **TOTAL TIME:** 30 minutes

---

3 slices bacon, cut into ¼-inch-wide pieces

6 cups chopped cabbage

½ cup chicken stock

1 tablespoon soy sauce, plus more to taste

1 teaspoon sesame oil

1. Add the bacon to the inner pot and heat on Sauté. Cook, stirring occasionally until browned, about 5 to 7 minutes. Press Cancel to stop the cooking.

2. Add the cabbage, stock, and soy sauce to the pot. Stir to combine.

3. Lock the lid. Cook on high pressure for 3 minutes, then manually release the pressure.

4. If there is too much liquid (and there probably will be with all of that cabbage), simmer on Sauté to reduce for a few minutes, stirring occasionally before mixing in the sesame oil. Season to taste with more soy sauce.

SUPER FAST
INSTANT POT
PRESSURE
COOKER
COOKBOOK

124

PICNIC BEAN SALAD

Picnic Bean Salad is a delicious combination of fresh and dried beans in a tasty vinaigrette. You could use canned beans, but dried taste so much better and the pressure cooker makes them a breeze to cook up. If you have fresh green beans from the garden, use them! Simply blanch them while the dried beans are cooking. **SERVES 6**

ACTIVE TIME: 10 minutes **PRESSURE TIME:** 8 minutes **RELEASE METHOD:** Natural (15 minutes) **TOTAL TIME:** 50 minutes (plus soaking overnight)

½ cup kidney beans, soaked overnight

½ cup black beans, soaked overnight

2½ cups water

½ teaspoon salt, plus more to taste

8 ounces frozen cut green beans, thawed and drained of excess liquid

1 red or green bell pepper, seeded and chopped

½ red onion, diced

1 clove garlic

½ teaspoon dried oregano

3 scallions, thinly sliced

½ cup olive oil

2 tablespoons red wine vinegar

Salt and pepper to taste

1. Drain and rinse the beans. Add them to the inner pot along with 2½ cups of water and ½ teaspoon of salt.

2. Lock the lid. Cook on high pressure for 8 minutes. Let the pressure release naturally for 15 minutes, then manually release any remaining pressure. Drain the beans in a colander.

3. Meanwhile, in a large bowl, stir together the green beans, bell pepper, onion, garlic, oregano, and scallions. Add the kidney and black beans, olive oil, vinegar, and salt and pepper to taste. Toss to combine.

SUPER-FAST TIP: Omit the garlic, oregano, olive oil, and vinegar, and substitute your favorite bottled vinaigrette.

TRADITIONAL COLLARDS

This Southern classic is usually cooked low and slow on the stove for at least an hour, but the pressure cooker makes delicious and tender collard greens doable in under 30 minutes. If desired, you can reduce the sauce, but don't discard it. This flavorful liquid, often called *pot likker*, is packed with vitamins. You could even use it instead of broth in another dish. **SERVES 4**

ACTIVE TIME: 10 minutes **PRESSURE TIME:** 6 minutes
RELEASE METHOD: Manual **TOTAL TIME:** 25 minutes

---

4 slices thick-cut bacon, chopped

5 cloves garlic, thinly sliced

1 pound collard greens, stems trimmed and leaves thinly sliced

1 cup chicken stock

2 teaspoons lemon juice

Kosher salt and black pepper

1. Heat the bacon in the inner pot on Sauté. Cook, stirring regularly until golden brown and crispy, about 5 to 7 minutes. Stir in the garlic and cook until fragrant, about 30 seconds. Press Cancel to stop the cooking.

2. Add the collards and stock, and stir to combine.

3. Lock the lid. Cook on high pressure for 6 minutes, then manually release the pressure. Add the lemon juice and salt and pepper to taste.

SUPER FAST
INSTANT POT
PRESSURE
COOKER
COOKBOOK

126

BASMATI RICE PILAF

Aromatic Basmati Rice Pilaf makes a simple but special side dish for any entrée you'd normally serve with plain white rice. To ensure fluffy rice, rinse the basmati well in a fine-mesh strainer until the water runs clear, so that all of the excess starch is removed. **SERVES 4**

ACTIVE TIME: 5 minutes **PRESSURE TIME:** 3 minutes
RELEASE METHOD: Natural (10 minutes) **TOTAL TIME:** 25 minutes

---

2 tablespoons unsalted butter

½ small onion, minced

1 cup basmati rice, rinsed

1¾ cups water

1 teaspoon salt

1. Heat the butter in the inner pot on Sauté. Add the onion and cook, stirring frequently until translucent, about 3 minutes.

2. Add the rice, and stir until well coated and toasted, another 1 to 2 minutes.

3. Stir in the water and salt.

4. Lock the lid. Cook on high pressure for 3 minutes. Let the pressure release naturally for 10 minutes, then manually release any remaining pressure.

SMART TIP: You can use stock instead of the water. If you do, reduce the salt to ¼ teaspoon. If it needs more salt, add it at the end.

SUPER FAST
INSTANT POT
PRESSURE
COOKER
COOKBOOK

128

SAFFRON RICE

Saffron may be one of the world's most expensive spices, but you only need a pinch of it to transfer big flavor and luminous color in this easy but impressive rice side. If you can, soak the saffron in hot stock beforehand to infuse even more of the spice's essence into the rice—and get the most bang for your saffron buck! **SERVES 4**

ACTIVE TIME: 5 minutes **PRESSURE TIME:** 3 minutes **RELEASE METHOD:** Natural (10 minutes) **TOTAL TIME:** 25 minutes (plus optional soaking time)

---

1 pinch (about 15–20 threads) saffron

1½ cups hot vegetable or chicken stock (see Smart Tip)

2 tablespoons olive oil or unsalted butter

½ small onion, minced

1 cup long-grain rice

¼ teaspoon salt

1 bay leaf (optional)

1. Time permitting, gently crush the saffron threads between your fingers and let them soak in the hot stock for up to 1 hour.

2. Heat the oil in the pot on Sauté. Add the onion and cook, stirring frequently until translucent, about 3 minutes.

3. Add the rice and cook until coated in the oil and translucent, another 1 to 2 minutes.

4. Add the stock with saffron, the salt, and a bay leaf (if using). Stir to combine.

5. Lock the lid. Cook on high pressure for 3 minutes. Let the pressure release naturally for 10 minutes, then manually release the pressure.

SMART TIP: The stock only needs to be hot if you are soaking the saffron. Otherwise room-temperature or refrigerated stock is fine.

CILANTRO LIME RICE

Liven up taco night with Cilantro Lime Rice. To make this dish spicy, add half a jalapeño to the food processor in step 3. **SERVES 4**

ACTIVE TIME: 5 minutes **PRESSURE TIME:** 3 minutes
RELEASE METHOD: Natural (10 minutes) **TOTAL TIME:** 25 minutes

---

1 cup long-grain rice

1½ cups vegetable or chicken stock

1 small garlic clove, minced

1 tablespoon extra-virgin olive oil

¼ cup lightly packed cilantro leaves

Juice of ½ lime, plus lime wedges for serving

Kosher salt

1. Add the rice and stock to the pot. Stir to combine.

2. Lock the lid. Cook on high pressure for 3 minutes. Let the pressure release naturally for 10 minutes, then manually release any remaining pressure.

3. Meanwhile, in a food processor, pulse the garlic, olive oil, cilantro, and lime juice until it is well blended. (You can also chop the ingredients by hand and mix them in a small bowl.)

4. Transfer the rice to a large bowl and add the cilantro mixture. Stir to combine. Season to taste with salt, and serve with lime wedges.

SUPER FAST
INSTANT POT
PRESSURE
COOKER
COOKBOOK

130

CREAMY MASHED BUTTERNUT SQUASH

You may not have thought of mashing butternut squash, but it makes a great and healthy alternative to regular mashed potatoes. **SERVES 4 TO 6**

ACTIVE TIME: 10 minutes **PRESSURE TIME:** 5 minutes
RELEASE METHOD: Manual **TOTAL TIME:** 25 minutes

2 pounds cubed butternut squash

2 tablespoons unsalted butter

1 teaspoon minced fresh thyme

1 tablespoon packed brown sugar

¼ cup heavy cream

Kosher salt and black pepper

1. Insert the steam rack into the multi-cooker and add 2 cups of water. Place a stainless-steel steamer basket (see page 11) on top of the rack and add the butternut squash.

2. Lock the lid. Cook on high pressure for 5 minutes, then manually release the pressure.

3. Transfer the squash to a large bowl and mash with a fork or potato masher.

4. Meanwhile, carefully remove the steamer basket and rack, and dump out the steaming water. Heat the butter in the now-empty pot on Sauté. Once it has melted, add the thyme and cook, stirring constantly until fragrant, about 30 seconds. Press Cancel.

5. Add the mashed squash, brown sugar, heavy cream, ½ teaspoon of salt, and ½ teaspoon of pepper to the pot, and stir to combine. Taste and adjust seasoning as needed.

MEDITERRANEAN QUINOA SALAD

Quinoa is a cinch in the pressure cooker. There's no need to bring it to a boil, lower the heat, and cover it, as you do on the stovetop. Just add the ingredients to the pot, lock the lid, and cook for a mere minute at high pressure. A long natural release ensures that it comes out perfectly cooked. You can *nearly* forget about it while you make the rest of dinner. **SERVES 4**

ACTIVE TIME: 10 minutes **PRESSURE TIME:** 1 minute
RELEASE METHOD: Natural **TOTAL TIME:** 30 minutes

---

1 cup quinoa

1½ cups vegetable stock or water

¼ teaspoon salt (if not using stock)

1 large tomato, seeded and chopped

½ red onion, diced

1 (4-ounce) jar sliced roasted red pepper, drained and cut into bite-sized pieces

1 small cucumber, peeled and diced

½ cup pitted oil-cured black olives (such as Kalamata), halved

1 (4-ounce) can corn, drained

2 teaspoons minced fresh oregano leaves, or ½ teaspoon dried

3 tablespoons extra-virgin olive oil

1 tablespoon lemon juice

5 ounces feta cheese, crumbled

Kosher salt and black pepper

1. Add the quinoa, stock, and salt (if needed) to the multi-cooker. Stir to combine.

2. Lock the lid. Cook on high pressure for 1 minute. Let the pressure release naturally.

3. Transfer the cooked quinoa to a large bowl, fluff it with a fork, and let it cool for 10 minutes.

4. To the same bowl, add the tomato, red onion, roasted red pepper, cucumber, olives, corn, oregano, olive oil, and lemon juice. Toss to combine. Gently fold in the cheese, and season with salt and pepper to taste. Serve warm or chilled.

SMART TIP: Feta is quite a salty cheese, so wait until after you've added it to the salad to decide whether the dish needs extra salt.

PESTO SPAGHETTI SQUASH

Spaghetti squash is a perfect fit for the pressure cooker and takes just minutes to prep. Then all you need to do is scrape out the squash strands and toss them together with herby pesto and sweet sundried tomatoes. **SERVES 4**

ACTIVE TIME: 5 minutes **PRESSURE TIME:** 4 minutes
RELEASE METHOD: Manual **TOTAL TIME:** 20 minutes

---

1 (approximately 3-pound) spaghetti squash, halved and seeded

3 to 4 tablespoons prepared pesto sauce

2 to 3 sundried tomatoes packed in oil, thinly sliced (optional)

Parmesan cheese, for serving

1. Insert the steam rack and add 2 cups of water to the inner pot. Add the spaghetti squash on top of the steam rack (see Smart Tip).

2. Lock the lid. Cook on high pressure for 4 minutes, then manually release the pressure. The strands should easily separate with a fork. If not, return to high pressure for another 1 to 2 minutes.

3. When the squash is cool enough to handle, use a fork and scrape the spaghetti-like strands out of the skin into a bowl.

4. Toss the squash with the pesto and sundried tomatoes (if using). If the dish is too thick, thin it out with a tablespoon of the steaming water. Serve with Parmesan cheese.

SMART TIP: If the spaghetti squash is very large, you may need to cut it into quarters to get it to fit. Just be sure to not fill the pot past the two-thirds full mark.

SUPER FAST
INSTANT POT
PRESSURE
COOKER
COOKBOOK

134

ASPARAGUS, TOMATO, AND FARRO SALAD

Fresh and hearty Asparagus, Tomato, and Farro Salad is an ideal make-ahead dish because it tastes better the next day after the flavors have had a chance to meld. It's also a great choice to pack as a work lunch. If you wish, you can stir in some chopped walnuts or cubed cheese to make it even more substantial.

SERVES 4

> **ACTIVE TIME:** 10 minutes **PRESSURE TIME:** 10 minutes
> **RELEASE METHOD:** Natural **TOTAL TIME:** 50 minutes (plus refrigerating time)

1 cup dry farro (choose the quicker-cooking semi-pearled variety)

Kosher salt and black pepper

4 cups water

½ pound asparagus, steamed and cut into 1-inch pieces

1 pint cherry tomatoes, halved

1 clove garlic, minced

3 tablespoons extra-virgin olive oil

1 tablespoon balsamic vinegar

2 tablespoons chopped fresh parlsey

1. Add the farro to the inner pot, along with 1 teaspoon of salt and the water.

2. Lock the lid. Cook on high pressure for 10 minutes. Let the pressure release naturally while you prepare the vegetables. When ready, the farro should be tender but still chewy.

3. Drain the farro, and transfer it to a large bowl. Toss it with the asparagus, tomatoes, garlic, olive oil, vinegar, parsley, and salt and pepper to taste.

4. Transfer the salad to the refrigerator to chill. Serve cold or at room temperature.

MAPLE "BAKED" BEANS

A sweet and savory favorite for picnics, these "baked" beans can be made in advance. **SERVES 4**

ACTIVE TIME: 15 minutes **PRESSURE TIME:** 6 minutes
RELEASE METHOD: Natural (15 minutes) **TOTAL TIME:** 45 minutes

---

½ pound small white beans, soaked overnight

1 tablespoon olive oil

Kosher salt and black pepper

4 slices bacon, chopped (optional)

1 onion, chopped

2 tablespoons mustard

¼ cup molasses

¼ cup maple syrup

2 teaspoons cider vinegar

1 tablespoon Tabasco sauce (optional)

1. Drain and rinse the soaked beans. Add them to the pot along with the oil, ½ teaspoon of salt, and enough water to cover the ingredients by at least an inch (do not fill the pot more than half full).

2. Lock the lid. Cook on high pressure for 6 minutes. Let the pressure release naturally for 15 minutes, then manually release any remaining pressure.

3. Meanwhile, in a large nonstick skillet over medium heat, add the bacon (if using) and onion, and cook until the bacon is browned and the onion is soft, about 7 to 10 minutes. Stir in the mustard, molasses, maple syrup, vinegar, and Tabasco sauce (if using). Season to taste with salt and black pepper. Remove the mixture from the heat, and set it aside.

4. Carefully drain the beans in a colander. Return them to the pot, along with the maple sauce and cook on Sauté, stirring frequently, for 5 minutes or until thickened.

SUPER-FAST TIP: Make the maple sauce while the beans cook!

SUPER FAST
INSTANT POT
PRESSURE
COOKER
COOKBOOK

136

ITALIAN GREEN BEANS

While the pressure cooker doesn't do crunchy well, it's perfect for these Italian-style green beans, which are braised in tomatoes and vegetable stock.

SERVES 4 TO 6

> **ACTIVE TIME:** 5 minutes **PRESSURE TIME:** 3 minutes
> **RELEASE METHOD:** Manual **TOTAL TIME:** 20 minutes

2 tablespoons extra-virgin olive oil, plus more for drizzling

4 cloves garlic, thinly slices

1 (14-ounce) can crushed tomatoes

½ cup vegetable stock or water

1½ pounds green beans, trimmed

Kosher salt and black pepper

¼ cup thinly sliced fresh basil

1. Heat the oil in the inner pot on Sauté. Add the garlic and cook, stirring frequently until lightly golden. Press Cancel to stop the cooking.

2. Stir in the tomatoes, stock, green beans, and salt and pepper to taste.

3. Lock the lid. Cook on low pressure for 3 minutes, then manually release the pressure.

4. If the sauce is too thin, cook it on Sauté for a few minutes until the desired consistency is reached, being sure not to overcook the beans.

5. Stir in the fresh basil, and drizzle the beans with more olive oil, if desired, before serving.

MAPLE-GLAZED CARROTS

These carrots would be equally tasty on the Thanksgiving table as they are in the middle of summer. Maple-Glazed Carrots are delicious with a simple squeeze of lemon juice. **SERVES 4**

ACTIVE TIME: 5 minutes **PRESSURE TIME:** 2 minutes
RELEASE METHOD: Manual **TOTAL TIME:** 20 minutes

1½ pounds carrots, peeled and cut into evenly sized pieces

1 cup water

Kosher salt and black pepper

2 tablespoons unsalted butter

1½ tablespoons maple syrup

1 teaspoon chopped fresh thyme leaves

Lemon wedges, for serving (optional)

1. Place the carrots, water, and 1 teaspoon of salt in the pot.

2. Lock the lid. Cook on high pressure for 2 minutes, then manually release the pressure. Drain the carrots in a colander.

3. Heat the butter in the inner pot on Sauté. When it's melted, add the carrots, maple syrup, salt and black pepper to taste, and thyme. Toss to coat. Press Cancel.

4. Serve with the lemon wedges (if using).

SUPER FAST
INSTANT POT
PRESSURE
COOKER
COOKBOOK

138

BALSAMIC BRUSSELS SPROUTS

A pressure cooker can be your best friend when it comes to preparing Thanksgiving dinner. You can make several side dishes in no time, including these Balsamic Brussels Sprouts, which may make their way into your regular side-dish rotation, as well. **SERVES 4 TO 6**

ACTIVE TIME: 10 minutes **PRESSURE TIME:** 5 minutes
RELEASE METHOD: Manual **TOTAL TIME:** 25 minutes

2 slices bacon, chopped

1½ pounds trimmed fresh Brussels sprouts

½ onion, thinly sliced

1 cup chicken stock

¼ cup shredded Parmesan cheese

2 tablespoons balsamic vinegar

1. Add the bacon to the inner pot and cook on Sauté, stirring frequently until browned. Using a slotted spoon, transfer the bacon to a paper towel–lined plate to drain.

2. Add the Brussels sprouts and onion and brown, stirring occasionally, 3 to 4 minutes. Stir in the chicken stock. Press Cancel.

3. Lock the lid. Cook on high pressure for 5 minutes, then manually release the pressure.

4. Transfer the sprouts to a serving dish. Toss them with Parmesan and the reserved bacon bits, and drizzle with vinegar.

SUPER FAST
INSTANT POT
PRESSURE
COOKER
COOKBOOK

140

GARLICKY PARMESAN BROCCOLI

This broccoli is meant to be soft and delicious, and so it works quite well under pressure. You can even spread it over crusty bread and drizzle it with olive oil.

SERVES 4 TO 6

ACTIVE TIME: 10 minutes **PRESSURE TIME:** 2 minutes
RELEASE METHOD: Manual **TOTAL TIME:** 25 minutes

¼ cup olive oil, plus more for drizzling

4 cloves garlic, minced

1 pinch red pepper flakes

½ cup vegetable stock

1½ pounds broccoli, trimmed into florets

½ cup grated Parmesan cheese

Kosher salt and black pepper

Lemon wedges, for serving

1. Heat the oil in the inner pot on Sauté. Add the garlic and red pepper flakes and cook until fragrant, about 30 seconds. Add the stock and broccoli and stir to combine. Press Cancel.

2. Lock the lid. Cook on low pressure for 2 minutes, then manually release the pressure.

3. Heat on Sauté for a few minutes to thicken the cooking liquid, then stir in the Parmesan. Season to taste with salt and pepper, and serve with lemon wedges.

SWEET
TREATS

DARK CHOCOLATE PUDDING

This pudding is a little richer than a regular chocolate pudding, so you may find yourself satisfied with just a small portion! Instead of fussing with individual ramekins, cook this in a single round baking dish. While this presentation may not be as personalized, it saves a great deal of time and energy! **SERVES 4 TO 6**

ACTIVE TIME: 20 minutes **PRESSURE TIME:** 15 minutes **RELEASE METHOD:** Natural (10 minutes) **TOTAL TIME:** 45 minutes (plus refrigerating time)

---

1 cup heavy cream

1 cup whole or 2% milk

4 ounces bittersweet chocolate, chopped

4 large egg yolks

½ cup packed light brown sugar

1 teaspoon vanilla

1 teaspoon instant espresso powder (optional)

¼ teaspoon kosher salt

Whipped cream, for serving

1. Insert the steamer rack in the inner pot and add 2 cups of water. Grease a high-sided 7-inch baking pan.

2. In a saucepan over medium heat, whisk together the heavy cream, milk, and chocolate, stirring constantly, until melted. Remove from the heat and set aside to cool slightly.

3. In a large bowl, whisk together the egg yolks, sugar, vanilla, espresso powder (if using), and salt.

4. Whisking constantly, add a small amount of the warm chocolate mixture to the egg yolk mixture. (This will help "temper" the eggs, so that they don't scramble.) Slowly continue adding the chocolate mixture, continuing to whisk until smooth. (If desired, you can strain the mixture through a fine-mesh strainer to ensure that the pudding is completely smooth and no egg or chocolate bits are left behind.)

SUPER FAST
INSTANT POT
PRESSURE
COOKER
COOKBOOK

144

5. Pour the mixture into the prepared pan and cover tightly with foil. Using a foil sling (see page 11), carefully lower the pan onto the rack and tuck in the foil ends.

6. Lock the lid. Cook on high pressure for 15 minutes. Let the pressure release naturally for 10 minutes, then manually release any remaining pressure.

7. Carefully remove the pan, uncover, and transfer to a wire rack to cool. When cool, transfer to the refrigerator to chill. Serve cold with whipped cream.

SMART TIP: The espresso powder helps boost the chocolate flavor, but you can omit it or substitute instant coffee granules, if you wish.

SIMPLE RICE PUDDING

Rice pudding can be a laborious affair, but this egg-free version really is as simple as can be. If you like raisins in your rice pudding, stir in a quarter cup in step 2, and they'll be nice and plumped up under pressure. The milk will split somewhat, but the addition of fresh cream plus the final stir will smooth everything out. **SERVES 6**

ACTIVE TIME: 10 minutes **PRESSURE TIME:** 8 minutes
RELEASE METHOD: Natural (10 minutes) **TOTAL TIME:** 40 minutes

---

1 tablespoon unsalted butter

1 cup medium- or long-grain rice

1¾ cups 2% milk

2 cups water

¼ cup packed light brown sugar

⅓ cup granulated sugar

Kosher salt

1 teaspoon vanilla extract

¼ cup heavy cream

Cinnamon, for serving

1. Add the butter to the inner pot and heat on Sauté. When the butter melts, add the rice, and stir until well coated and slightly translucent, about 1 to 2 minutes. Press Cancel.

2. Add the milk, water, brown sugar, granulated sugar, and ½ teaspoon of salt, and stir to combine.

3. Lock the lid. Cook on low pressure for 8 minutes. Let the pressure release naturally for 10 minutes, then manually release any remaining pressure.

4. Carefully open the lid. If the pudding is too thin, press Sauté and cook, stirring constantly until slightly thickened, but keep in mind that the dish will thicken substantially upon cooling. Press Cancel and stir in the vanilla and heavy cream.

5. Serve warm, room temperature, or cold, with a sprinkle of cinnamon.

SUPER FAST
INSTANT POT
PRESSURE
COOKER
COOKBOOK

146

"BAKED" APPLES

Baked apples are a favorite fall dessert, but you might not have thought of "baking" them in the pressure cooker. If you wish, add some crushed pecans or walnuts to the stuffing mixture. These apples are perfect with a scoop of vanilla ice cream. **SERVES 4**

ACTIVE TIME: 5 minutes **PRESSURE TIME:** 3 minutes
RELEASE METHOD: Natural (10 minutes) **TOTAL TIME:** 25 minutes

---

¼ cup raisins

⅓ cup packed brown sugar

¼ cup softened unsalted butter

½ teaspoon cinnamon

1 pinch nutmeg (optional)

4 baking apples, such as Granny Smith, Golden Delicious, or Winesap, cored

1. Add 2 cups of water to the inner pot and insert the steam rack. Lightly grease a high-sided 7-inch round baking pan.

2. In a small bowl, mix together the raisins, sugar, butter, and cinnamon. If desired, add a little grated nutmeg as well.

3. Place the apples in the prepared pan and stuff evenly with the sugar mixture. Cover the top with foil.

4. Using a foil sling (page 11), transfer the pan to the pot and tuck in the foil ends.

5. Lock the lid. Cook on high pressure for 3 minutes. Let the pressure release naturally for 10 minutes, then manually release any remaining pressure.

6. Serve warm, spooning the sauce on top.

SUPER FAST
INSTANT POT
PRESSURE
COOKER
COOKBOOK

148

APPLES AND CINNAMON STEEL-CUT OATS

What's the biggest obstacle when it comes to making steel-cut oats? It's time, right? That's 20 to 30 minutes you have to stand at the stove, stirring and watching a pot. Very few people can spare half an hour in the morning as they get ready to face the day. Although this recipe doesn't shave much off the total cooking time (it's still about 30 minutes start to finish), only about 2 or 3 minutes of that requires your full attention. Steel-cut oats do need a long natural release, allowing you plenty of time to get ready for work!

Don't omit the butter as it will help reduce foaming; however, you could substitute coconut oil if you prefer. For added flavor and nutrition, top the finished oatmeal with cubed fresh apple, crushed pecans or walnuts, and a splash of milk. Leftovers can be refrigerated for another breakfast. **SERVES 4**

ACTIVE TIME: 3 minutes **PRESSURE TIME:** 3 minutes
RELEASE METHOD: Natural **TOTAL TIME:** 30 minutes

---

1 tablespoon unsalted butter

1 cup steel-cut (not quick-cooking) oats

3 cups water

¼ teaspoon kosher salt

½ teaspoon cinnamon

⅓ cup chopped dried apple

¼ cup packed dark brown sugar

1. Add the butter to the inner pot and heat on Sauté. Once the butter has melted, press Cancel to stop the cooking.

2. Add the oats, water, salt, cinnamon, apple, and brown sugar. Stir to combine.

3. Lock the lid. Cook on high pressure for 3 minutes. Allow the pressure to release naturally. Stir and serve.

VARIATION: For maple and brown sugar oatmeal, omit the cinnamon and apple and drizzle with maple syrup to serve.

WHITE WINE-POACHED PEARS

The key to perfect poached pears is making sure the pears are ripe, but not too soft. **SERVES 4**

ACTIVE TIME: 5 minutes **PRESSURE TIME:** 5 minutes
RELEASE METHOD: Natural (10 minutes) **TOTAL TIME:** 30 minutes

---

1 (750 milliliter) bottle white wine

1 cup sugar

1 stick cinnamon

1 tablespoon vanilla extract

Juice of 1 lemon

Juice of 1 orange

1 bay leaf (optional)

4 Bartlett pears, peeled, halved, and cored

1. To the inner pot, add the wine, sugar, cinnamon, vanilla, citrus juices, and bay leaf (if using). Heat on Sauté, and stir until the sugar dissolves.

2. Place the pears in the pot, and submerge them as much as possible in the sugar syrup.

3. Lock the lid. Cook on high pressure for 5 minutes. Let the pressure release naturally for 10 minutes, then manually release the remaining pressure.

4. Stir the pears to coat fully in syrup. Eat plain with syrup spooned on top, or top with vanilla ice cream or yogurt before serving.

CHERRY CHEESECAKE

If you're new to using a pressure cooker, you may be slightly surprised at the idea of making a cheesecake in it, but pressure cookers are actually quite well known for turning out fabulous cheesecakes. A cheesecake may break the under-sixty-minutes rule, but it's worth it. In fact, it may even serve as a gateway into making many more cheesecakes, because it's smaller than a regular cheesecake (not too many tempting leftovers!) and you don't have to mess around with a hot water bath. Like most cheesecakes, this one is even better the next day, after it's had a chance to firm up in the refrigerator. It has just a hint of lemon flavor that pairs well with the cherry topping. **SERVES 6**

ACTIVE TIME: 20 minutes **PRESSURE TIME:** 30 minutes **RELEASE METHOD:** Natural
TOTAL TIME: 80 minutes (plus cooling and refrigerating time)

4 ounces (about 1 cup) graham cracker crumbs

3 tablespoons unsalted butter, melted

2 (8-ounce) packages cream cheese, at room temperature

½ cup sour cream, at room temperature

½ cup sugar

1 tablespoon all-purpose flour

½ teaspoon lemon zest

1½ teaspoons lemon juice

1 teaspoon vanilla extract

2 large eggs, plus 1 egg yolk, at room temperature

Jarred sour cherries in syrup, for serving

1. Insert the steamer rack and add 2 cups of water to the pot. Grease a 6-inch springform pan.

2. In a small bowl, stir together the graham cracker and butter until the crumbs are moistened. Press the crumbs firmly into the bottom of the prepared pan. Refrigerate while you proceed with the rest of the recipe.

3. Using a handheld or stand mixer, blend together the cream cheese, sour cream, sugar, flour, lemon zest and juice, and vanilla extract until smooth. Add in the eggs, one at a time, and blend until combined.

4. Scrape the mixture into the prepared pan. Wrap the bottom of the pan with foil to prevent spills, and cover the top with aluminum foil. Using a foil sling (see page 11), lower the pan into the pot and tuck in the ends of the foil.

SUPER FAST
INSTANT POT
PRESSURE
COOKER
COOKBOOK

152

5. Lock the lid. Cook on high pressure for 30 minutes. Let the pressure release naturally.

6. Carefully transfer the pan to a cooling rack, and remove the foil top to allow any condensation to evaporate. Let the cake cool for at least 1 hour. Refrigerate until cold, about 3 hours. Serve topped with cherries and their syrup.

SALTED CARAMEL CHEESECAKE

Creamy and sweet with a crunchy touch of flaky sea salt, Salted Caramel Cheesecake will make your cheesecake dreams come true. Don't forget to drizzle it with extra caramel sauce before serving! **SERVES 6**

ACTIVE TIME: 20 minutes   **PRESSURE TIME:** 30 minutes
RELEASE METHOD: Natural   **TOTAL TIME:** 80 minutes

---

4 ounces (about 1 cup) graham cracker crumbs

3 tablespoons unsalted butter, melted

2 (8-ounce) packages cream cheese, at room temperature

½ cup sour cream, at room temperature

¼ cup sugar

1 tablespoon all-purpose flour

¼ cup prepared caramel sauce, such as dulce de leche (see Smart Tip), plus more for garnish

1 teaspoon lemon juice

1 teaspoon vanilla

½ teaspoon sea salt, plus flaky sea salt for serving

2 large eggs, plus 1 egg yolk, at room temperature

1. Insert the steamer rack and add 2 cups of water to the pot. Grease a 6-inch springform pan.

2. In a small bowl, stir together the graham cracker and butter until the crumbs are moistened. Press the crumbs firmly into the bottom of the prepared pan. Refrigerate while you proceed with the rest of the recipe.

3. Using a handheld or stand mixer, blend together the cream cheese, sour cream, sugar, flour, caramel sauce, lemon juice, vanilla, and ½ teaspoon of salt until smooth. Add in the eggs, and blend until combined.

4. Scrape the mixture into the prepared pan. Wrap the bottom of the pan with foil to prevent spills, and cover the top with aluminum foil. Using a foil sling (see page 11), lower the pan into the pot and tuck in the ends of the foil.

5. Lock the lid. Cook on high pressure for 30 minutes. Let the pressure release naturally.

SUPER FAST
INSTANT POT
PRESSURE
COOKER
COOKBOOK

154

6. Carefully transfer the pan to a cooling rack, and remove the foil top to allow any condensation to evaporate. Let cool for at least 1 hour, then refrigerate until cold, about 3 hours. Serve drizzled with more caramel sauce and sprinkled with a pinch of flaky sea salt.

SMART TIP: You can often find dulce de leche with the Latin foods in the international aisle of your grocery store. If you can't find it, just substitute another prepared caramel sauce, which is usually located near the ice cream toppings or jams.

CHOCOLATE BREAD PUDDING

Few desserts combine frugality and deliciousness in the way that bread pudding does. It's a perfect use for stale bread. Serve Chocolate Bread Pudding warm with a scoop of vanilla ice cream. **SERVES 4 TO 6**

ACTIVE TIME: 20 minutes **PRESSURE TIME:** 20 minutes
RELEASE METHOD: Natural (10 minutes) **TOTAL TIME:** 60 minutes

---

½ stick (¼ cup) unsalted butter

4 ounces chopped bittersweet chocolate

½ cup sugar

3 large eggs

2 to 2½ cups whole milk or half-and-half

1 teaspoon vanilla extract

2 tablespoons rum

4 heaping cups cubed stale white bread

SMART TIP: You can use either whole milk or half-and-half. Half-and-half will give you a richer, more decadent dessert.

1. Insert the steamer rack in the inner pot and add 2 cups of water. Grease a high-sided 7-inch round baking pan.

2. In a small saucepan over low heat, melt the butter and chocolate, stirring constantly. Remove the mixture from the heat, and let it cool slightly.

3. In large bowl, whisk together the sugar, eggs, 2 cups of the milk, the vanilla, and the rum. Add the cooled chocolate mixture to the egg mixture, and whisk to combine. Add the bread cubes, and press them down into the liquid. Let the bread mixture sit a few minutes to allow the bread to soften and absorb the liquid. If the mixture seems dry, add more milk, up to the remaining half cup.

4. Transfer the mixture to the prepared pan and cover tightly with foil. Using a foil sling (see page 11), carefully lower the pan into the pot, tucking in the ends.

5. Lock the lid. Cook on high pressure for 20 minutes. Let the pressure release naturally for 10 minutes, then manually release any remaining pressure. Serve either warm or cold.

SUPER FAST
INSTANT POT
PRESSURE
COOKER
COOKBOOK

156

RICH CRÈME BRÛLÉE

Crème brûlée is one of those classic desserts you imagine will appear in front of you at a nice French restaurant, or exclusively on a special occasion. This high-end reputation must mean that it's incredibly difficult to make. Not so! In just a short time, you can prepare tasty crème brûlée in your multi-cooker and have a beautiful dessert on the table for any occasion—whether it's special or just your average weeknight. **SERVES 4**

ACTIVE TIME: 5 minutes **PRESSURE TIME:** 10 minutes
RELEASE METHOD: Manual **TOTAL TIME:** 25 minutes

6 egg yolks

2 cups heavy cream

7 tablespoons sugar, divided

1 teaspoon vanilla extract

1. Insert the steamer rack in the inner pot and add 2 cups of water.

2. In a 4-cup measuring cup or medium bowl, whisk together the egg yolks, heavy cream, 5 tablespoons of the sugar, and vanilla extract until combined.

3. Pour mixture into 4 ramekins and cover each with foil. Place the ramekins in the pot.

4. Lock the lid. Cook on high pressure for 10 minutes, then manually release the pressure.

5. Remove the ramekins from the pot. Remove the foil and allow to cool in the fridge for several minutes.

6. Once cool, sprinkle the sugar on top of each. Broil for 1 minute or use a kitchen torch to caramelize the tops.

SMART TIP: Use a 4-cup measuring cup to mix the main ingredients. The lip allows you to pour the mixture into the ramekins without causing a mess.

INDEX